THE JOURNALING GYM

START, RESTART, AND STICK TO THE MOST POWERFUL HABIT FOR YOUR MIND

RAJIV KRISHNAN PISHAROTI

ISBN
Paperback 979-8-89906-999-4
Hardcase 979-8-89984-213-9

Contents

Foreword

In a world that glorifies Achievement over Awareness, we often forget the importance of Pausing, Reflecting, and truly Listening to ourselves. We are taught how to chase success, but rarely how to sit with ourselves, process our emotions, and cultivate inner peace. The Journaling Gym would serve as a much-needed companion — for every seeker on the journey inward.

What *Rajiv Pisharoti* offers here is more than just a book — it is a mirror reflecting presence, peace, and *path to profound self-awareness.* He has created a space where thoughts meet honesty, where emotions find expression, and where strength is built not in silence, but in self-conversation. This is not about grammar, perfection, or poetic sentences. It is about being real, being raw. And above all, being kind to ourselves.

As someone who believes in the profound power of swa-chintan (self-reflection), I deeply resonate with the essence of this book. Just as meditation is a mirror for the soul, journaling — as Rajiv presents it — is a mirror for the mind. The emotional workouts, the thoughtfully designed prompts, and the real stories within these pages make it more than a journal. It becomes a spiritual tool — one that brings Awareness, Acceptance, and ultimately, Transformation!

To all who turn these pages: You are not alone in your questions or your silent battles. With every entry, you're not merely writing — you're healing, transforming, and finding your way back home to yourself.

My blessings to Rajiv and to all readers of The Journaling Gym. May it serve as your companion on the path of self-discovery, strength, and peace.

Love and Light,

Rajyogi Brahmakumar Nikunj

Spiritual Mentor, Popular Columnist with over 9000 Published Columns in 4 Languages and National Coordinator of Media Wing of Brahma Kumaris

Introduction:
Why This Book, Why Now

Personal story

For over a decade, I've worked in the field of learning & development—sometimes as a trainer representing a firm, and at other times as an in-house L&D lead. In all that time, one question has echoed through nearly every meeting, pitch, or post-training conversation:

"What happens after training?"

I remember clearly, years ago, pitching a soft skills program—on management development—to the HR head of a respected company. She listened patiently, nodded at the right places, and even acknowledged the relevance of the topic. But then she leaned back and asked:

"How will we measure its impact?"

I gave her the standard responses. We talked about feedback forms, pre- and post-assessments, behavioural changes, and so on.

But she wasn't satisfied.

Her response was training sessions often create a spark—participants feel energized, motivated, even transformed—but that spark fades quickly once they return to their daily routines. The momentum rarely lasts, and the insights gained during training are often forgotten or pushed aside by everyday pressures.

Needless to mention, I didn't get that business. Over time, I faced similar rejections many a times.

Clients weren't being difficult—they were being realistic. Training involves money, and in most organizations, any such expense needs to be justified—ideally with measurable outcomes.

Whether I was working for a training company or managing L&D within an organization, the core concern remained the same:

How do we make learning sustainable?

How do we move beyond the "high" of a workshop and turn learning into a personal, continuous habit?

That's when a deeper question began to take root in my mind—not just as a professional, but as a learner myself:

What does self-driven, everyday learning look like?

I began to realize, it's also about an habit that's been my quiet companion for over a decade. A habit I believe can make learning—and life richer, more intentional, and far more joyful — through a quiet habit that's been by my side for years: **"journaling."**

In fact, in today's digital age, many know what it is—and even aware of its benefits. Yet, only a fraction of people actually practice it consistently.

This gap between knowing and doing was what made me write this book.

How Journaling Transforms Others

We all have days when we feel like we're running on autopilot — doing, reacting, achieving, but never really arriving anywhere meaningful. In such times, journaling becomes more than a habit. It becomes a **homecoming**.

And the best part? You don't have to be a writer to start. You just have to be **willing to be honest**.

I've seen people come to journaling from all walks of life — CEOs, students, teachers, new parents, retirees, artists, and engineers. Some start because a therapist or coach suggested it. Some pick up the habit after a painful breakup, a career shift, or a phase of deep questioning. And others, surprisingly, begin simply out of curiosity.

But almost all of them discover something they didn't expect: a new kind of **clarity**.

They begin to notice how writing helps them **slow down the noise** in their minds. How naming an emotion helps **soften its grip**. How, after a few weeks, a little quiet scribble on a page becomes a conversation with the self — a lifeline they come to cherish.

Journaling is a space to:

- **Start**, even if you've never done it before.

- **Restart**, if you've dropped the habit (like we all do sometimes).

- And most importantly, **stick with it** — in a way that feels natural and doable in daily life.

In my own work, I've watched people journal their way through self-doubt, grief, burnout, confusion, anxiety — not to magically erase the struggle, but to **make sense of it**. To hold space for it. And in doing so, to emerge more centered, more whole.

One young leader I worked with said, *"I started journaling when I didn't know what I wanted from my career. Now I still don't have all the answers — but I'm asking better questions."*

Another, an artist in her 60s, told me, *"Journaling is how I learned to speak kindly to myself again."*

These aren't isolated stories. They're quiet revolutions happening in notebooks across the world.

Journaling won't give you instant solutions. It won't erase pain. It won't make life simpler. But what it will do is **build something lasting**:

A stronger, wiser, more compassionate relationship with your own thoughts.

And in that relationship lies the power to **make better choices**, understand yourself more deeply, and **grow** — every single day.

So wherever you're starting from, you're in the right place.

No pressure. No rules. Just **you**, your thoughts, and the page.

Let this be your space. Let this be your beginning. More importantly Let's begin !

Reader Promise

You didn't pick up this book by accident.

Something in you is seeking a pause. A breath. A way to make sense of the thoughts that swirl in your mind — some loud, some quiet, some whispering in the corners of your day. Maybe you've tried journaling before, maybe this is your first time. Maybe you've kept secrets in notebooks, or maybe writing feels like a stranger. Either way, this book is for you.

I promise you this:

By the time you finish this book, journaling will no longer feel like a mystery or a luxury — it will feel like a *necessity*, a tool, and most importantly, *a friend*. You will see how a simple notebook can become a therapist's couch, a personal coach, a mirror, a map — sometimes all at once.

But more than that, you'll have a clear, structured, and sustainable method — a Journaling Gym — that trains your emotional muscles, builds mental clarity, and cultivates self-awareness in just a few minutes a day. No fluff. No pressure. Just honest words and powerful outcomes.

This book is not about writing beautifully. It's about writing truthfully. It's not about being productive — it's about being present.

It's not even about journaling, really.

It's about *you*. Showing up. Every day. Even for five minutes.

And here's my deeper promise: If you commit to this practice — even imperfectly — you'll begin to notice shifts.

- You'll see patterns in your thinking.
- You'll understand your emotional weather.
- And slowly, you'll feel more anchored — not because the storm outside stopped, but because you found stillness within.

Let this book be your companion, your coach, and your quiet motivator. Not all pages will feel easy. Not every prompt will feel necessary. But trust the process. Trust *yourself*.

You've already begun the most important part — showing up.

How to Use This Book

This is not a book you need to read from start to finish in one go — it's a book you **work with**, much like how you'd show up at a gym.

Each chapter has been designed like a **station** in your journaling workout — with concepts, insights, and prompts that help you stretch your mind, tone your awareness, and strengthen your emotional resilience.

You can read a chapter a week or spend longer. You can reread sections that hit home or skip ahead to what calls you today. There's no one correct way to journal — only the honest way.

Every chapter ends with **practical journal prompts** and **thought exercises** you can engage with directly. All you need is a pen, sometime carved out for yourself, and the willingness to be open.

Some readers might want to **start journaling right away** using the prompts. Others might want to **read a few chapters first** before putting pen to paper. Both are fine. This is your gym. Your pace. Your practice.

Here's how to get the most out of this book:

- 📖 **Read with a pen nearby** – underline what resonates, scribble notes in the margins.

- 📔 **Create a journaling routine** – whether it's 10 minutes each morning or a weekly check-in, consistency trumps intensity.

- ✍ **Use the Journal Gym Prompts** – every chapter includes guided prompts to help you reflect and write.

- 🔄 **Revisit key ideas** – this book isn't just for a one-time read. Come back to the exercises, especially during life's noisy seasons.

💬 From the Author

When I first began journaling, I had no idea it would become one of the most powerful tools in my life. Over the years, I've turned to the page in moments of confusion, celebration, heartbreak, and healing. What began as a survival tool became a way to thrive — and today, it's one of my greatest sources of calm.

This book is built on what I've learned through years of practice and through guiding others on this path. I've seen how writing can transform how we think, feel, relate, and lead.

I would like to believe it will do the same for you.

— Rajiv Krishnan Pisharoti

A Quick Note Before We Begin

In the pages ahead, you'll meet some familiar names — from **Oprah Winfrey** to **Barack Obama**, **Leonardo da Vinci** and more. Every mention is drawn from publicly available sources — interviews, memoirs, speeches, or published writings — and is intended solely to illustrate how journaling has quietly supported even the busiest, brightest minds.

None of these individuals have endorsed this book — but their stories continue to inspire, and I've included them here to remind us all of what's possible when we simply return to the page.

Every care has been taken to present these references accurately and respectfully, in the spirit of illustrating the impact and universality of journaling. These individuals have been mentioned as examples, not as contributors or endorsers of this book. If any errors of representation have inadvertently occurred, I welcome correction with humility and gratitude.

— Rajiv Krishnan Pisharoti

✎ Your Turn: A Gentle Beginning

"Now that you've heard my 'why,' it's time to find your own. Let's begin your journaling journey — one page at a time."

Before we go any further, let's begin right here. Gently. Just you, the page, and a pen.

Prompt: What's your relationship with journaling?

Have you ever journaled before?

If yes, what did it feel like?

If no, what's stopped you?

Try writing one sentence that captures your thoughts about journaling. For example:

"I don't know if I can keep up with journaling."

or

"Journaling felt like a friend I didn't know I needed."

Chapter 1

The Case for Journaling Gym

Marie Bashkirtseff was an Ukrainian-French artist in the 19th century. She began journaling at the age of 13—not for fame, not for school, not even for personal development in the modern sense. She wrote because she needed a place to express, to process, and to be truly herself.

There were no fancy prompts. No digital reminders. No journaling communities. Just one person, a pen, and the need to make sense of her inner world.

She never imagined her writing would go beyond her own eyes.

But after her untimely death, her journals were discovered and published.

And what emerged wasn't just a collection of private thoughts—it was one of the most celebrated personal journals of all time. Readers across countries and generations found themselves, in her raw honesty, in the questions she asked, in the vivid way she captured life as it was unfolding.

What started as a private, personal space later became one of the most insightful and celebrated journals ever published.

Her journal, titled *Journal de Marie Bashkirtseff*, was published posthumously in 1887, and later translated into English in 1889 as *Marie Bashkirtseff: The Journal of a Young Artist 1860–1884*. Today, her writing offers a rare and intimate glimpse into the mind of a young woman navigating art, ambition, and identity in a complex world.

Source: Wikipedia – Marie Bashkirtseff

Read the journal: HathiTrust Digital Library

She didn't set out to create a masterpiece. She simply started. And that's all you need to do, too.

You don't need a grand plan. You don't need to write beautifully. You don't need to know where it will lead.

You just need to start.

Because the act of journaling—like going to the gym—isn't about perfection. It's about consistency. It's about giving your thoughts a space to breathe. A place to land.

And who knows? Maybe one day, years from now, you'll look back at your own words and realize you were writing the story of your own growth, one page at a time.

However before we begin, let's take a moment to understand what journaling does to ourselves. To begin with our mind.

What Journaling Really Does for Your Mind

"You don't have to be a writer to journal. You just have to be a human being willing to listen to your own mind."

In 1942, a 13-year-old girl in Amsterdam received a red-and-white checkered diary for her birthday. Her name was Anne Frank. Like many teenagers, she began filling its pages with thoughts about school, friendships, and daily life. But as her world changed dramatically—forced into hiding with her family to escape Nazi persecution—so did her writing.

That diary became something far more powerful: a lifeline, a place of reflection, a quiet rebellion against despair. Page by page, Anne preserved not just the facts of her days, but the **voice of her inner world**—full of curiosity, fear, insight, and hope. She journaled through some of the darkest times imaginable, and in doing so, she remained connected to herself.

After her death, that same diary was discovered, published, and went on to become *The Diary of Anne Frank*—one of the most iconic and widely read books of the 20th century. Translated into over 70 languages, it continues to move generations of readers. But its origin was simple: one girl, one notebook, and the act of sitting down to write.

Anne Frank never set out to write a "famous" book. She just wrote to understand her thoughts, to hold on to hope, and to survive—mentally and emotionally.

That is the quiet power of journaling.

We've all heard it before—journaling is good for you.

But why?

Is it just another mindfulness trend, another feel-good habit we try for a week and forget? Or is there something more fundamental at play?

Here's what I've come to believe:

Journaling is not just a self-care ritual.

It is **mental fitness.**

As vital as brushing your teeth or moving your body. Not urgent, but essential.

You don't need to do it for hours. You don't even need to be good at it.

You just need to show up.

Because when you write, you **don't just empty your mind—** you **organize** it.

You **don't just describe your thoughts—**you **catch them mid-flight,** before they spiral into stress.

You **don't just vent—**you **listen** to the quiet truths beneath the noise.

This isn't about becoming the next Anne Frank or Marie Bashkirtseff.

It's about becoming more **you—**clearer, calmer, and more connected to what's going on inside.

Journaling isn't magic. But it does something quietly radical. It makes you pay attention to yourself. Not in a self-indulgent way, but in a deeply human one.

It gives you a few sacred minutes each day to say,

"This is what I'm carrying. Let me look at it."

And in those minutes, your mind exhales.

It sounds simple — pick up a pen, write a few lines. But what if I told you that journaling isn't just writing… it's like taking a deep breath for your brain?

Let's start with the most immediate thing it does — it declutters your mind.

Journaling as Mental Decluttering

We live in a world of tabs — open tabs on our browser, and open tabs in our minds. Things left unsaid, undone, unprocessed. Journaling is how we start closing them, one by one.

Imagine this:

You're working with 14 tabs open on your laptop. One is a half-written email. Another is a bill you meant to pay. Yet another is a tab you opened just to look up something — and never did.

You feel restless. Scattered. Not because any one task is overwhelming —

but because they're *all* unfinished.

Now imagine your **mind** is the same. Tabs open from yesterday's conversation. From last year's breakup. From dreams you shelved. Thoughts that return when you're trying to sleep. Questions that buzz faintly in the background.

That's cognitive clutter.

And journaling?

That's how you start hitting **close tab** — one entry at a time. No need to solve everything.

Just name it. Sit with it. Let it out.

You'll be amazed how much lighter your mind feels — and how much clearer your next step becomes.

"Your mind is for having ideas, not holding them."

— *David Allen* (Author of *Getting Things Done*)

But once the mind feels lighter — once you've begun closing those mental tabs — something remarkable happens. You start to notice what keeps reopening them.

Journaling doesn't just help you unload. It helps you understand.

Because when you show up to the page regularly, patterns begin to show up too.

That's when journaling stops being a toolbox and starts becoming a mirror.

Journaling as a mirror -

Journaling doesn't just help you offload — it holds up a mirror. As you flip through pages, you begin to notice: "Why am I always anxious on Sundays?" "Why do I shrink myself in meetings?" Patterns emerge. And with them, power.

Leonardo da Vinci: The Genius Revealed Through Ink

Leonardo da Vinci — one of history's most celebrated **polymaths** (*a person with wide-ranging knowledge or learning across many fields*) — is often remembered for his artistic masterpieces such as *The Last Supper, Vitruvian Man,* and of course, the enigmatic *Mona Lisa,* whose mysterious smile has intrigued generations.

But Leonardo wasn't just an artist. He was also a scientist, an engineer, an architect, an anatomist, and an inventor — and behind all of this brilliance was a quiet, relentless habit that helped unlock his genius: **journaling**.

Over his lifetime, Leonardo filled more than **7,000 pages** of notebooks. These journals were not orderly treatises or carefully organized collections. They were wild and untamed — overflowing with sketches, musings, mathematical formulas, diagrams of inventions, and even grocery lists. On one page, you might find an intricate drawing of a flying machine; on another, a humble reminder to "buy vinegar." One moment, he's observing how a bird lands, and the next, he's scribbling thoughts about human emotion, the flow of water, or the mechanics of the heart.

To the casual observer, his journals may seem chaotic — even incoherent. But within this apparent disorder was profound clarity.

Through his journaling, Leonardo began to spot patterns — not just in the world around him, but within himself. He noticed how he kept returning to certain obsessions: the movement of water, the anatomy of the human body, the possibility of human flight. His repeated sketches and notes on these themes weren't random. They were reflections of deep, enduring curiosities.

Over time, these fascinations shaped the direction of his work. His relentless study of human anatomy led to the *Vitruvian Man* — a perfect blend of art and science. His observations of light, shadow, and emotion found expression in the haunting smile of *Mona Lisa*. His sketches of birds and bats laid the conceptual groundwork for flying machines that predated the airplane by centuries.

Journaling, for Leonardo, wasn't just a record of thoughts. It was a process of **self-discovery**. It was through this daily act of writing and sketching — of questioning and reflecting — that he made sense of the world and of himself. His journals helped him not only to remember, but to recognize — to see what truly mattered, what fuelled his creativity, and what questions kept tugging at his mind.

In that sense, journaling didn't just **document** his genius — it **revealed** it.

Interestingly, **his journals were never intended for publication**. They were deeply personal and largely unknown to the world until **centuries later**, when they were compiled and published posthumously. Today, they are known by titles like **"The Notebooks of Leonardo da Vinci"**, and individual compilations such as **"The Codex Leicester"** — which was famously purchased by Bill Gates in 1994 for over $30 million — stand as proof of the enduring power of a curious mind on paper.

Leonardo's messy, magical notebooks remind us that clarity doesn't come from tidiness, but from **truthful expression.**

"I have been impressed with the urgency of doing. Knowing is not enough; we must apply. Being willing is not enough; we must do."

— *Leonardo da Vinci*

"But once we recognize a pattern, the question becomes — what now?"

It's here that the pen shifts from being a mirror to becoming a compass — helping us steer through emotional storms with grace and clarity

Regulating Emotions Through the pen

Marcus Aurelius: A Stoic's Pen in the Eye of the Storm

Marcus Aurelius — Roman Emperor, philosopher, warrior — ruled over one of the greatest empires in history during a time of immense turmoil. From relentless wars on the frontiers to plague outbreaks in Rome, from personal betrayals by those closest to him to the unimaginable burden of leading millions — Marcus lived in a constant state of pressure and uncertainty.

Yet amid the chaos of the Roman court and the brutality of battlefield camps, Marcus found solace in an unlikely place: the pages of his private journal.

In the quiet hours of early morning or the stillness after long, demanding days, Marcus would write. He did not write for an audience, for scholars, or for legacy. He wrote for himself. These reflections — never intended to be published — were his way of staying grounded in a world that threatened to unravel him.

What we now know as *Meditations* was, in truth, a deeply personal collection of thoughts — fragments of philosophy, self-reminders, and quiet questions. They weren't grand proclamations or political manifestos. They were **mental handrails**, something to hold onto when the waves of life threatened to sweep him away.

Marcus was a **Stoic** — not just in temperament, but in philosophy. **The word "Stoic" refers to someone who remains calm and unemotional, especially in difficult situations.** But for Marcus, Stoicism wasn't about suppressing feelings — it was about understanding them and responding wisely.

Stoicism, the ancient Greek philosophy he followed, teaches that we cannot control what happens to us, but we can always control how we respond. It values calm over chaos, reason over reaction, and inner peace over external noise.

In the midst of overwhelming grief after the loss of children, during moments of deep fatigue in war camps, and while facing the betrayal of close allies, Marcus didn't explode or retreat. He **picked up his pen**. Instead of reacting outwardly, he reflected inwardly.

He would write to himself questions like:

- "Is this in my control?"
- "What would a wise man do in this situation?"
- "How much time will I waste worrying about what others think?"

Through these pages, Marcus practiced what we now call **emotional regulation** — not by ignoring emotions or bottling them up, but by meeting them head-on, honestly and without drama.

Journaling became his way of sifting through emotion to find **principle**, of transforming anxiety into perspective, and of reminding himself that **how he responded** was always within his power, even when circumstances were not.

And so, as fires of rebellion burned, as friends turned into foes, and as the empire groaned under the weight of plague and war — Marcus kept writing. Each page was a pause. Each entry was a recalibration. Each word helped him return to the still center within himself.

Centuries later, these private writings would be compiled into what we now call *Meditations* — a timeless guide to resilience, self-discipline, and inner peace. It remains one of the most revered books in the history of philosophy and has guided presidents, athletes, generals, and thinkers for generations.

Marcus teaches us that even at the height of power, the greatest battles are the **internal ones**, and the pen can be the most effective sword.

"You have power over your mind — not outside events. Realize this, and you will find strength."

— *Marcus Aurelius, Meditations*

From Ancient Scrolls to Modern Struggles

Marcus Aurelius wrote to survive the storms of empire — not for glory, but for grounding. Centuries later, another leader, navigating a different kind of turbulence, would also turn to the pen — not as a philosopher-king, but as a young man trying to make sense of identity, purpose, and belonging. The circumstances had changed, but the instinct remained: when the world becomes too loud, write to hear yourself

From Chaos To Clarity

The Barack Obama Story

Before the world knew him as the 44th President of the United States, Barack Obama was a young man navigating layers of internal conflict. As a child of a Kenyan father and a white American mother, raised in Hawaii and Indonesia, he carried within him questions that didn't have easy answers: *Who am I? Where do I belong? What am I meant to do in this world?*

In his twenties and thirties, long before the spotlight, Obama often found himself overwhelmed — not by the lack of opportunities, but by the overabundance of thoughts, expectations, and self-doubt. He wasn't yet a senator or a national figure. He was a community organizer in Chicago, earning little, trying to make a difference, and wondering if any of it mattered.

It was during these years that he began to write. Not policy papers or campaign speeches — just thoughts. Reflections. Fragments of ideas. Doubts. Fears. Dreams. Sometimes they came as letters never sent. Sometimes as journal entries in notebooks that no one else would read.

He once described this process in his memoir *"Dreams from My Father"* — how writing became a space to sort through the chaos in his head. He didn't write to solve problems directly, but to better understand *himself.* Why he reacted a certain way. Why he was drawn to justice. Why certain memories stuck with him and others didn't.

He wasn't seeking answers in the traditional sense. He was trying to see. Journaling helped him do just that — to separate the noise of ambition from the voice of purpose. The very clarity he would one day be admired for in his speeches was first cultivated in the quiet, unpolished pages of his journal.

Years later, when he had to make weighty decisions as President — decisions that would affect millions — he returned to that same reflective space. Even in the White House, amidst advisors and analysts, he would step back to write, to think, and to feel. Journaling helped him not just react, but respond with clarity and integrity.

"Writing is a form of therapy; sometimes I wonder how all those, who do not write, compose or paint can manage to escape the madness, the melancholia, the panic and fear which is inherent in a human situation."

— Graham Greene

Journaling as Self-Therapy

"Not everyone can afford a therapist — but everyone can hold a pen. Journaling offers an intimate space for emotional release, where the act of naming what we feel can soften its grip."

Hugh Jackman is a name synonymous with global stardom. From the adamantium-clawed Wolverine in *X-Men* to his Oscar-nominated performance in *Les Misérables*, Jackman has carved a career that spans action, drama, musicals, and Broadway — earning a Tony Award, an Emmy, a Golden Globe, and a Grammy along the way. He's a versatile performer, known for his magnetic stage presence and emotional depth, admired by millions across the world.

But behind the curtain of success and accolades lies a deeply human story — one that many can relate to but few talk about openly. Jackman grew up in Sydney, Australia, the youngest of five children. When he was just eight years old, his mother left the family and moved to England — an event that left a lasting emotional scar. Though outwardly successful, he often battled with feelings he didn't fully understand — anxiety, self-doubt, unresolved grief — tucked beneath his larger-than-life public persona.

It was later in life, at the height of his career, that Jackman began to acknowledge the need for deeper self-care. While he had achieved the kind of fame most actors dream of, internally, he struggled with regulating his emotions and maintaining mental balance, especially under the intense spotlight of celebrity life.

In interviews, including one with *Vanity Fair*, Jackman spoke about how his therapist suggested a simple practice: journaling. It wasn't about writing something profound — it was about creating a space each day to check in with himself. To let the noise out. To articulate what was going on beneath the surface. And in doing so, he found something unexpected: relief.

Journaling gave Jackman a way to sift through emotions he didn't always have words for in conversation. Whether it was frustration, fear, or fatigue — he could put it on paper, and suddenly it didn't have the same power over him. The process allowed him to slow down, observe himself without judgment, and reflect on his responses to life's many demands.

He began each morning with a few quiet moments, pen in hand, tuning into his thoughts before the world rushed in. Over time, this practice helped him build emotional awareness and resilience — not by ignoring his struggles, but by confronting them with honesty and compassion.

As Jackman himself put it, journaling became an anchor — a private space where he could return to himself, day after day. For someone known for portraying powerful, often emotionally complex characters on screen, this behind-the-scenes ritual became an essential tool for personal growth and mental health.

And Hugh Jackman is not alone. His story is a reminder that even those who seem the most confident and successful often need help making sense of what's going on inside. Journaling doesn't promise to fix everything, but it does offer a safe, accessible way to begin. To unpack. To breathe.

Because as Jackman discovered — and as many others continue to discover — the simple act of writing can become one of the most powerful acts of healing.

Journaling as a resilience

In a world that constantly demands emotional agility, mental clarity, and inner strength, **resilience is no longer optional**. While earlier sections gently introduced journaling as a tool for self-awareness, this section goes deeper. Why? Because resilience isn't a one-time decision — it's a *daily practice*. And journaling is one of the simplest yet most powerful ways to cultivate it.

Journaling: Not Just Reflection, But a Lifeline

When chaos strikes — whether externally in the form of loss or trauma, or internally as anxiety or burnout — journaling becomes more than an emotional outlet. It becomes a **container**, a safe space where we process pain, untangle fears, and make meaning out of disorder.

Let's look at how people in real life — across generations and geographies — have used this simple act of writing to not only survive but heal and grow.

Case 1: Viktor Frankl – Journaling Without Paper

During his imprisonment in Nazi concentration camps, psychiatrist **Viktor Frankl** mentally composed what would later become his seminal book *Man's Search for Meaning*. He didn't have a pen or paper — but he journaled in his mind. He clung to the mental exercise of recording his reflections, the small acts of kindness he witnessed, and the meaning he could find in the suffering.

This internal journaling kept him anchored to his identity and humanity. He later wrote:

"Everything can be taken from a man but one thing: the last of the human freedoms—to choose one's attitude in any given set of circumstances."

His story proves: even the idea of journaling — of creating a narrative — can be a profound tool of resilience.

Case 2: The 9/11 Firefighter Who Wrote Through Grief

After the 9/11 attacks, a New York firefighter named **John** (name anonymized in a published piece in *The Atlantic*) began journaling each night. At first, he wrote just one sentence:

"I'm still alive, but I don't feel alive."

But over weeks and months, those single sentences turned into paragraphs — and eventually into a ritual. Through writing, he found space to release guilt, confusion, and trauma. He didn't try to be eloquent. He just tried to be honest.

Years later, in a public interview, he said:

"I didn't go to therapy. I didn't talk much. But that notebook? That was my therapist."

Case 3: Syrian Refugee Children – Finding Peace in Pages

In refugee camps across Lebanon and Jordan, several NGOs have introduced **journaling workshops** for displaced Syrian children. These children — many of whom have lost homes, schools, and even family — are invited to write stories, memories, or drawings in a private notebook.

A 12-year-old girl named Noor wrote:

"Today I remembered the jasmine tree near our house. I drew it. It made me smile."

That act of remembering — and capturing it — brought her temporary peace. In a setting defined by uncertainty, journaling became a small ritual of control and hope.

The Science That Supports It

Dr. **James Pennebaker**, a leading psychologist, has extensively studied **expressive writing**. His research shows that writing about traumatic or emotionally significant experiences — even for just 15 minutes a day — leads to:

- Decreased cortisol levels (stress hormone)
- Improved immune function
- Better sleep
- Faster recovery from physical injuries

Pennebaker says:

"When people write about emotional upheavals, they begin to organize and structure the experience. It turns chaos into a narrative."

That structure is resilience.

The Power of Looking Back

One overlooked aspect of journaling is **rereading** old entries. When someone revisits pages written in grief, rage, or fear and realizes how far they've come — that's proof of survival. That's resilience.

A woman who journaled through her divorce once shared:

"Reading my journal now, I don't even recognize that woman. But I'm proud of her. She fought. She healed. She became me."

"You may not control all the events that happen to you, but you can decide not to be reduced by them."

— *Maya Angelou*

From Modern Pages to Ancient Scrolls

If today's journals are building inner strength, it's worth asking: **how did people in ancient times manage stress, self-doubt, or crisis — without apps, therapy, or even books?** The answer: they *wrote*. They inscribed, they etched, they reflected — on papyrus, parchment, or in sacred texts. The medium has changed, but the *need* to write remains timeless.

From Ancient Scrolls to Now: A Timeless Practice

Journaling might look modern — filled with aesthetic notebooks, productivity hacks, and #Gratitude hashtags — but it is one of humanity's oldest inner technologies. Across civilizations, we've always used writing not just to remember but to *make sense* of things: of ourselves, of loss, of triumph, of faith, and of fear.

While earlier sections of this work may have offered a quick sketch of journaling's purpose, I wish to dwell on this in greater detail. Because here lies something profound: a practice that is simple but sacred — where private writing has held space for some of the most public transformations in history.

Let us explore five powerful real-life examples across time and culture that illuminate this timeless practice.

Case 1: The Egyptian Scribe's Tablet (2000 BCE)

Among the ruins of Luxor in Egypt, archaeologists found a small clay tablet that surprised them. Instead of records of trade or taxation — common for that period — this tablet had a far more intimate tone. It described the thoughts of a young student, likely an apprentice scribe. The writing was unpolished, even grammatically flawed — but deeply human.

He described being chastised by his teacher, the long hours spent copying hieroglyphs by torchlight, and his secret wish to return home. This wasn't a logbook. It was emotional processing. It was a child's struggle written in clay.

This single piece of writing changes how we view history. It reminds us that **journaling predates literature**. People didn't wait for printing presses to explore their inner lives. Even then, under the weight of dynasty and discipline, someone carved their **truth** into clay. For no one else. Just themselves.

It's the oldest known example of personal reflection in written form — 2,000 years before paper existed.

Case 2: The Dead Sea Scrolls — Faith Meets Private Reflection (150 BCE)

Often considered one of the most important archaeological finds of the 20th century, the **Dead Sea Scrolls** were discovered in the Qumran Caves of Israel in 1947. Among religious texts and legal codes, scholars also found personal reflections and prayers of individuals believed to be part of a monastic Jewish sect called the Essenes.

What stood out wasn't just the theology, but the emotional honesty. One scroll contains a passage where a man confesses his personal doubts:

"I am a vessel of clay, cracked and leaking. But I write, so that I may not forget that the Lord fills even the empty jar."

This isn't doctrine. It's despair, hope, and longing expressed with quiet vulnerability. **Even in sacred texts, we find journaling — private emotion woven into spiritual life.**

What this tells us is that journaling wasn't just about coping — it was often about *belonging*. About anchoring oneself in values when the world was uncertain. For the Essenes, writing was their lifeline to God — and to themselves.

Case 3: Li Qingzhao – Grief and Grace in Song Dynasty China (12th Century)

Li Qingzhao, a poet and noblewoman from the Song Dynasty in China, lived a life of profound personal loss. After her husband's death and the fall of her city to war, she lost not just her home but her entire literary collection — over 10,000 books and manuscripts.

Displaced and grieving, she turned inward. Her journal entries, written in a blend of poetry and prose, are heartbreakingly honest. She wrote not just about politics or art, but about how it felt to wake up alone. About forgetting the sound of her husband's voice. About guilt, survival, and how even tea lost its taste.

"I tried to read tonight. But even the ink feels cold."

What makes Li's writings powerful is that they weren't meant for anyone. They were grief, scribbled by candlelight — in a time when women's voices were rarely preserved.

Li's work — some of it found centuries later in temple archives — continues to inspire Chinese writers today. She showed that journaling could be **grace in motion**. A way of holding on when the world is falling apart.

Case 4: The War Diary of Mihail Sebastian – A Romanian Jew Under Fascism (1935–1944)

Mihail Sebastian was a Romanian playwright and intellectual who kept a detailed journal during the years of growing antisemitism and fascism in Europe. His journal, discovered and published posthumously in the late 20th century, is now considered one of the most haunting personal documents of the Holocaust era.

In his entries, he documents the betrayal of friends who turned against him, the casual normalization of hate in the streets of Bucharest, and his own internal breakdowns — not because he feared death, but because he felt invisible. Forgotten.

"I write so I can exist. If no one sees me, this journal does."

He writes not as a historian but as a man trying not to disappear — trying to keep his *sense of self* intact in a world that refused to see him as human.

The diary ends abruptly in 1944, shortly before Sebastian was killed in a street accident — just as the war was ending. His journal stands today as proof of one thing: **writing privately can be an act of resistance**.

Case 5: The Journals of May Sarton — Ageing, Solitude, and Inner Seasons (20th Century)

American poet and novelist **May Sarton** used her journals to explore the emotional terrain of ageing, solitude, creativity, and inner conflict. Her book *"Journal of a Solitude"* (1973) reads like a slow walk through her thoughts — sometimes hopeful, sometimes angry, often quiet.

She reflected not just on external events, but on how those events touched her internally — the loneliness after friends left, the guilt of snapping at someone she loved, the joy of tending her garden.

Unlike Anne Frank or Marcus Aurelius, Sarton published her journals in her lifetime. But even then, they weren't written for an audience. They were meditations — on being human.

"I write to learn what I'm thinking," she says.

"I write to understand what I feel."

For many, her journals became a mirror. Proof that we don't write in journals because we have the answers — we write because **we're willing to sit with the questions**.

Linking the Past to the Present

So what connects an Egyptian apprentice, a grieving Chinese widow, a Romanian Jew, and a solitary American poet?

They had nothing in common — except this: **They wrote to survive.**

Emotionally.Spiritually. Psychologically.

They didn't always know who they were. But writing helped them find out.

From sacred scrolls to private grief notes to published diaries, journaling has always been an act of resilience. It helps us preserve what is disappearing — be it a memory, a sense of self, or the feeling of being alive in a particular moment.

So when we open our notebook today — in the era of apps and AI — we're not starting a trend.

We're continuing a **4,000-year-old human tradition**.

Prompt: Can journaling be your daily mental workout?

Just like your body needs a little movement every day, your mind does too. Journaling is like a gentle gym for your thoughts. You don't need big feelings or fancy words — just a few lines a day can build emotional strength.

Chapter Summary:
Gathering the Threads: A Pause to Reflect

This chapter sets the emotional and practical foundation for the journaling journey ahead.

Through personal anecdotes and lived experiences in the learning & development space, I have tried to confront a familiar and frustrating truth: traditional training often sparks change, but that spark quickly fades. The deeper question arises — how can we make learning *sustainable*?

The answer, i discovered, lies in a simple yet profound habit: **journaling**. Not as a tool of productivity or perfection, but as a space for presence, truth, and clarity.

I saw how journaling transforms lives — from professionals navigating career confusion, to artists reconnecting with themselves. The power of putting thoughts to paper is not in the answers it gives, but in the questions it awakens.

The chapter invites the reader with warmth and honesty:

- You don't need to be a writer.
- You don't need to do it "right".
- You just need to show up — imperfectly, consistently.

Finally, it offers a **reader promise**: this is not just a book, but a companion. Through prompts, reflections, and gentle guidance, you will build a habit that strengthens your emotional awareness, mental clarity, and self-trust. And all it takes is a few quiet minutes a day.

This is your space. Your pace. Your beginning.

✐ Your Turn: Let's try a 5-day journaling workout.

Write just 3–5 lines each day. That's it.

📇 **Day 1** – *What's one thing on your mind right now?*

It could be something exciting, stressful, or even boring. Write it down honestly.

📇 **Day 2** – *What made you smile recently?*

Big or small. A person, a message, a moment — write it down.

📇 **Day 3** – *What are you avoiding?*

Be gentle. Say it without judgment. Notice how your body feels when you write this.

📇 **Day 4** – *What's one thing you wish had done differently this week?*

Write what happened — and what you learned from it.

📇 **Day 5** – *Write a message to your future self.*

Even 3 lines are okay. You can say "keep going," "don't forget to rest," or whatever you need to hear.

You don't have to show it to anyone. You just have to show up. That's how resilience is built — one small line at a time.

Chapter 2

Starting from Scratch

Overcoming the First Blank Page

It stares at you, daring you to begin. The fresh notebook. The clean screen. The untouched journal page.

You bought the book. You carved out the time. You're finally ready to build the journaling habit everyone keeps talking about. And yet, when you sit down to write your first entry — nothing comes. Your mind goes blank. Your pen hovers. The page remains empty.

Sound familiar?

Welcome to what is, arguably, the biggest psychological hurdle in journaling — the blank page.

You're not alone. In fact, nearly everyone who has ever tried journaling (including authors, artists, CEOs, and students) has faced this very moment. It isn't about a lack of ideas. It's about the pressure we put on ourselves in that very first moment of creation.

We want to get it right. We want the first entry to mean something. To look good. To reflect who we are. We want it to be clear, intelligent, maybe even a little profound.

But here's the truth: **it doesn't need to be any of that.**

The first page doesn't need to be poetic. Or wise. Or even interesting.

It just needs to exist.

Let's explore why the blank page is so intimidating — and how to get past it.

1. The Perfection Illusion

We often place too much importance on beginnings. It's why people delay launching a business, writing a book, or starting therapy. We think the start has to be amazing. We think the tone we set will determine the entire journey.

But journaling isn't a movie with a first scene. It's more like a trail walk. You take a step and then another. Some are muddy. Some are beautiful. But they all lead somewhere.

And your journal? It doesn't need a polished beginning. It needs an honest one.

The antidote? **Lower the bar.**

Try writing just three words.

Try writing the date.

Try writing, "I don't know what to write."

That's not failure. That's entry.

The goal is not to impress, but to express.

You've just started. Congratulations!

2. The Fear of Exposure

Many people don't realize that part of the blank page fear comes from a sense of vulnerability. "What if someone finds this?" "What if I sound ridiculous?"

These are valid thoughts. Journaling is personal, and even the idea of exposing one's thoughts — even to oneself — can be uncomfortable.

Sometimes the scariest person to be honest with is you.

Creating safety can look like this:

- Choosing a journal that feels private — perhaps digital, with a password.
- Writing in code words, metaphors, or nicknames.
- Starting with mundane observations — the weather, your coffee — until your heart feels ready to speak.

Remind yourself: *This is not a performance. It's a space.*

You don't have to share it. You may not even reread it, even though it's very good to do so.

You just have to release it.

3. You Don't Need a Plan

Another myth: you need a structured approach from day one. A theme. A format. A goal.

Not true.

Your first entry can be:

- A list of things on your mind.

- A few sentences about your day.

- A conversation with yourself.

One powerful prompt to try is:

"What do I need to hear today?"

This is how self-trust begins — by giving yourself space to answer questions no one else asks you.

Start messy. Stay open.

You're not writing for clarity. You're writing to find it.

4. Letting Go of the Audience

The moment we imagine someone else reading our words, we censor ourselves. We perform. We write for approval.

Journaling is your rebellion against that.

It is the rare place where you can:

- Drop the act.

- Ramble.

- Repeat.

- Contradict yourself.

Let your journal be your place to exhale.

There's no applause coming. That's the gift.

5. Movement Creates Momentum

The blank page loses its power the moment your pen moves.

Just start writing. Anything. Describe what's in front of you. Talk about the weather. The coffee. The awkward conversation you had yesterday.

The mind loves inertia. Once it sees motion, it stops resisting.

Before you know it, thoughts begin to appear. Words surface. Patterns emerge. You're no longer writing — you're in flow.

Start small, and let momentum take care of the rest.

6. Real-Life Examples

- **Arianna Huffington**, founder of *The Huffington Post*, once wrote about how her first journal entry after years of not writing was simply: "Today was too much. I'm tired." That entry opened the floodgates for reflections that became the basis of her bestselling book *Thrive*.

- **Tim Ferriss**, author of *The 4-Hour Workweek*, uses what he calls "morning pages" to clear mental fog. His rule: write three pages, even if it's just the word "I don't know what to write" repeated for a paragraph.

- **Lady Gaga** journals her way through overwhelm and anxiety. Her early entries are, in her own words, "chaotic and confusing." But out of that chaos, she finds insight. "Journaling lets me meet myself — and some days, that's the hardest part."

7. Your First Entry Can Be a Letter

Try writing a letter:

- To your future self.

- To a younger version of you.

- To someone you'll never send it to.

Begin with:

"Dear Me, I don't know how to start this. So I'm just going to write whatever comes out."

(You may discover truths you didn't know you were holding.)

8. You Are Not Late

There's a strange pressure we put on ourselves when it comes to starting something new — especially something personal, like journaling. We wait for the right notebook, the right time of year, or the right "mental space." We tell ourselves, "I'll start on Monday," or "once things settle down."

But let's be honest: life rarely settles down. And perfect timing is often just perfectionism in disguise.

The truth is: **you are not late.**

Not because others started years ago. Not because you bought that notebook three months ago and haven't touched it. Not because you once tried journaling and stopped. You are here now — and that is enough.

Every journey starts with a messy first step. The value of journaling doesn't come from starting "on time." It comes from showing up — today, just as you are.

Write this down right now if you need to:

☞ *"I am not behind. I am beginning."*

You don't need to fill pages. You don't need to catch up. You don't need to "be consistent" before you even start. You just need to write something — today. Even if it's one line.

Start small. Start scared. Start scribbling.

But start.

Because that blank page is not a test. It's an invitation.

An invitation to pause.

To be real.

To listen to your own voice.

To breathe.

"Start where you are. Use what you have. Do what you can."

— Arthur Ashe

Let this be your moment. Let this be your beginning.

You're not late. You're right on time.

9. The Myth of the "Right Mood"

One of the most subtle traps in journaling is waiting for the "right mood" to write.

We tell ourselves we'll journal when we feel calm, when the house is quiet, when we're inspired — and suddenly, days turn into weeks without a single word written. But here's the reality: the right mood rarely arrives on its own. Most days come packed with noise, distractions, and fatigue. And if you wait for the perfect moment, you might never begin.

The secret? **Write in the mood you're in.**

Grumpy? Let it out.

Tired? Say so.

Anxious? Describe the feeling.

Unmotivated? Scribble: "I don't feel like doing this, but I'm here."

By showing up in your *real* emotional state, you're giving your journal what it was made for: honesty. Some of the most authentic, healing entries are written not in peace, but in chaos.

Don't journal *because* you're clear — journal *to become* clear.

Just like a runner doesn't stretch because they feel loose, but to get loose, your pen is the stretch. Writing invites the right mood — it doesn't wait for it.

"Discipline is choosing between what you want now and what you want most."

– Abraham Lincoln

10. When Words Don't Work, Try Doodles

Sometimes, the page feels blank because your brain doesn't want to use words.

And that's okay.

Who said journaling had to be paragraphs and punctuation?

Try this:

- Draw a spiral and write how your day spun out of control.
- Sketch a timeline of your morning.
- Use arrows, boxes, bubbles — like a mind map.
- Create a comic strip of your mood.

Some people process better visually than verbally. Doodling lets your subconscious speak without language. Over time, patterns still emerge — just in shapes instead of sentences.

And sometimes, your heart just needs to scribble.

One executive I worked with used to draw a sun, clouds, or a thunderstorm each morning to reflect his mood — no words. After three months, he could track emotional patterns just by flipping through the symbols.

The point isn't artistic merit. It's expression.

Let your journal be your playground. Your sketchpad. Your mess.

When the blank page doesn't welcome words, answer with color, with lines, with symbols. Let your pen wander.

Sometimes the most profound clarity comes from what we draw when we're done trying to write.

"Creativity is intelligence having fun."

– Albert Einstein

11. The Myth of Having Nothing to Say

One of the biggest misconceptions is, "I don't have anything to write about." But the truth is, every single day gives you material — your thoughts, feelings, memories, doubts, tiny wins, or even what annoyed you while brushing your teeth.

You may not have a "big idea," but you have **real moments**. And that's more than enough.

In fact, some of the richest entries come from the smallest observations:

- "I didn't enjoy my lunch today — maybe I was distracted."
- "I felt really peaceful while waiting at the signal."
- "Why do I feel nervous when my phone rings?"

These aren't grand revelations. But they are **anchors to awareness**.

When you think you have nothing to say, try this:

- What's something that surprised me today?
- What emotion have I carried around most?
- If my mind was a room right now, what would it look like?

Still blank?

Write: *"I feel blank because…"* and finish the sentence.

Still struggling?

Write: *"What I wish I could tell someone right now is…"*

You'll soon realize you're never actually empty. You're just **unwarmed**. And journaling is how you start that fire.

"If you wait until you feel like writing, you're going to wait a long time."

— *Lemony Snicket*

12. Journaling Doesn't Have to Start with Words

You don't always need sentences to begin a journal entry. Sometimes, **lists** are the perfect bridge into your thoughts. They reduce pressure and get the pen moving.

Try these:

- 5 things I noticed today
- 3 moments that made me smile
- 4 thoughts looping in my mind
- 2 things I'm grateful for
- 1 thing I want to let go of

Lists are quick, doable, and low-stakes. They don't need grammar. They don't need structure. And yet, they hold tremendous emotional insight.

Here's what often happens: You start with a short list and suddenly, one point wants to expand into a paragraph. That's your subconscious stepping forward. That's your inner self saying, "I'm ready now."

Even doodle lists work. Circle your energy level. Rate your mood from 1 to 10. Sketch arrows for what drained you vs. what energized you.

And if even that feels hard, try one line:

"Today I want to write, but I don't know where to begin."

That one sentence *is* your beginning.

You don't need a plan. Just a pen.

"Don't wait for the muse. She has a lousy sense of timekeeping."

— Barbara Kingsolver

(The phrase suggests that if you sit around waiting for inspiration to magically arrive, you'll probably be waiting a long time — because the muse is notoriously **unreliable and late**.)

13. Begin with Borrowed Words

When your own words won't come, begin with someone else's.

Use a quote, a line from a book, a lyric from a song, or even a sentence you overheard. Start there — and let it spark a reaction, a memory, a question.

Here's how it might look:

- Quote: "You can't pour from an empty cup."
- Response: "I think that's where I've been living lately — half-full, pretending to overflow."

Or try a lyric:

- "I'm a survivor, I'm not gonna give up."
- Response: "That line makes me emotional. I don't always feel like a survivor. Today was heavy."

Borrowed words are **doorways**. They remove the pressure to "be original." And they remind you that someone, somewhere, has already voiced something close to what you feel.

Sometimes we just need a hand to hold — even if it's from a line in a book.

Try these journal prompts:

- "A quote I needed to hear today…"

- "What this lyric reminds me of…"

- "Someone once said… and it stuck with me."

Journaling isn't about invention. It's about connection.

Start with someone else's voice… and watch how your own begins to speak.

"Books are mirrors: you only see in them what you already have inside you."

— Carlos Ruiz Zafón

You've cracked the hardest part — you faced the blank page and wrote anyway. Whether it was one sentence, one list, or a doodle of your cat with stress issues, you showed up. And that's the win.

But now that you've taken the first step, let's talk about something that gets surprisingly overlooked: **the tools**. Because while journaling is mostly about what's on your mind, the *how* and *where* you write can make or break the habit.

So let's dig into pens, pages, apps, and atmospheres — and help you build a toolkit you actually look forward to using.

Choosing Your Tools

Or: How to Make the Pen Mightier Than Procrastination

Let's be honest — one of the biggest reasons people don't journal consistently isn't a lack of time or thoughts. It's because the pen skips. Or the app feels sterile. Or the notebook is "too pretty to ruin."

Yes, really. Tools matter more than we think.

✏️ 1. The Notebook Paralysis

Raise your hand if you've ever bought a gorgeous notebook… and then refused to write in it because it felt "too nice." 🧑‍🎨 🔮

This is a classic journaling dilemma. You stand in a stationery store, lovingly run your fingers over a Moleskine or a handmade journal, and think: *"This is the one. This is the notebook that will finally make me reflective, wise, and mildly mysterious."*

Then you bring it home and… nothing. It stays untouched on your shelf. Because you don't want to mess it up.

Solution? Get over the idea of "ruining" it. The value of a journal isn't in the pages — it's in what *you* put there. Scribble, cross out, spell badly. The mess *is* the magic.

"A journal is not a museum. It's a construction site."

— Anonymous (but possibly your inner voice)

Also, consider having two journals: one "nice" one for reflective entries, and a "rough" one where you can brain-dump without guilt.

▦ 2. Analog vs. Digital: The Great Debate

There are strong opinions in this space. Some people swear by ink-on-paper. Others prefer the speed and convenience of typing.

Here's the truth: both work. And both have pros and cons.

Writing by hand slows your thoughts, anchors you in the moment, and engages your brain differently. Studies even suggest it improves emotional processing and memory.

But **digital journaling** has benefits too:

- It's searchable.
- It's private (hello, password protection).
- It's quick — great for busy mornings or mid-meeting venting.

☞ **Pro tip:** If you're not sure which suits you, try this:

- Morning = write by hand (to slow down).
- Evening = type it out (to clear your mind faster).

You can also mix it up: use a note-taking app during the day, and transfer highlights into your physical journal at night.

Some popular digital tools:

- **Day One (iOS/Mac)** – sleek, secure, and tag-friendly.
- **Journey (Android/iOS)** – easy to use and cloud-backed.
- **Google Docs/Notion** – for the minimalists and organizers.

✎ 3. Pen Talk: It's More Important Than You Think

If journaling feels physically awkward, it might be your pen's fault.

That free hotel pen? It was never meant for greatness.

A good pen glides. It feels just right in your fingers. You look forward to using it. It makes your words feel worthy, even if you're venting about the fact that you overcooked rice again.

Fan favorites:

- **Pilot** – smooth, reliable, inexpensive.
- **Uniball** – if you like clean lines with zero smudge.

You don't need to go full "pen connoisseur" — just find one that brings a little joy when you hold it. That's your pen.

⬡ 4. The Journaling Space

You don't need a meditation room with a Himalayan salt lamp (though hey, if you've got it, own it).

But having a *go-to* space really helps.

Your journaling space should be:

- **Comfortable** (but not nap-inducing).
- **Accessible** (not buried under laundry).
- **Lightly ritualized** (a candle, a playlist, or even just a consistent mug of chai).

I know one person who journals at the same café every Thursday morning — same corner table, same cappuccino. It's her ritual. That physical routine helps anchor her mental one.

Create a vibe that says: *"I'm here for me."*

📅 5. Time of Day: When to Journal

There's no "right" time, only *your* time.

Morning journaling gives you clarity and intention. It's a great way to set the tone for your day.

Evening journaling helps you download emotions and thoughts, reflect, and reset.

Some people journal twice a day — a quick check-in in the morning, and a deeper entry at night.

Pick a time when:

- Your mind is relatively free.
- You're less likely to be interrupted.
- You can show up consistently, even if for just 5–7 minutes.

Pro tip: pair it with an existing habit (e.g. right after brushing your teeth or with your first coffee).

🎒 6. Your Starter Kit (Optional But Fun)

Here's a quick journaling "starter pack" that won't break the bank and still feels like a treat:

- 1 decent notebook (not too fancy, not too flimsy)
- 2 pens you enjoy writing with
- 1 journaling space (your desk, a café corner, your car parked under a tree)
- 1 reminder (sticky note, alarm, calendar block)

- 1 small object that makes the space yours (a quote card, crystal, keychain, whatever speaks to you)

These small signals create consistency — which builds comfort — which leads to flow.

◉ Real-Life Example: The Dented Diary

A friend of mine, bought a beautiful leather-bound journal from an airport bookstore. She never wrote in it. It just sat there like a museum piece for months.

One day, she spilled coffee on it by accident. Furious, she considered tossing it — but then thought, "It's ruined now anyway."

That day, she wrote her first entry. It wasn't deep — just a rant about a long queue and her ruined bag. But it felt freeing. She's now on her fourth journal.

Moral of the story? The coffee stain was the best thing that ever happened to that notebook.

📝 A Gentle Nudge

If you've struggled to be "consistent" in the past, don't blame your motivation. It might just be your tools.

Find tools that make you smile, not sigh.

Let your pen feel like a friend.

Let your journal feel like a room that's always open — lights dim, music soft, just waiting for you to return.

"The tools we choose can whisper encouragement — or stay silent. Choose the ones that speak back."

— Rajiv Krishnan Pisharoti

So now you've picked your tools — whether it's a hand-stitched leather journal, a scrappy notepad, or a password-protected app. You've got a pen you like, a cozy nook or a good café corner, and you've even resisted the temptation to hoard beautiful notebooks you're too afraid to "ruin."

Now comes the moment you've probably been both looking forward to and secretly dreading: **your first entry**.

But here's the secret:

Your first entry doesn't have to be perfect. It just has to be **yours**.

Let's explore what that first step looks like — through awkward beginnings, honest words, and even some delightfully messy first pages of people you've probably heard of.

Let's be real — the first page of any journal carries an odd pressure.

It stares back at you, all blank and expectant, like a new haircut waiting to be complimented.

We feel this weird need to *"start strong."*

To say something profound.

To write like we're Shakespeare channeling Brené Brown.

But the truth is, **your first entry doesn't need to be deep. It just needs to be true.**

📖 Real-Life First Entries: Not So Perfect, But So Human

Let's take a peek into history for some reassurance.

🧠 **Marcus Aurelius**, Roman emperor and stoic philosopher, didn't start *Meditations* by proclaiming eternal wisdom. His early entries were simple reminders — notes to himself like:

"Be tolerant with others and strict with yourself."

That's it. That's how one of the most revered philosophy books in history started — like a post-it stuck to his own soul.

🧒 **Anne Frank** began her now-iconic diary with:

"I hope I will be able to confide everything to you... and I hope you will be a great source of comfort and support."

Sweet. Tentative. Like a girl writing to a pen pal she hadn't met yet — which, in a way, she was.

🎨 **Leonardo da Vinci**, the original multitasker, opened some of his early pages with to-do lists.

Things like:

- "Buy vinegar"
- "Ask about the sun"
- "Draw Milan Cathedral"

His entries weren't lofty essays. They were curiosities. Observations. Tasks. Scribbles.

Your first page doesn't need to win a Pulitzer.

It just needs to break the silence.

🧶 So, What Should You Write?

The shortest, truest answer: **Whatever you want.**

Here are a few gentle starters:

- "Today, I decided to start journaling. I don't know why exactly, but I'm curious."
- "Here's what's on my mind right now…"
- "I feel ___ today. I'm not sure why, but maybe writing will help."
- "If this journal were a person, I'd tell it…"

Even:

"I have no idea what to write, but I'm showing up. That's something."

✦ That is something. That is *everything*.

😄 First Entry Fails (That Turned Out Just Fine)

Let's inject some humor here.

A friend of mine once began her new journal with:

"Okay. This is dumb. I'll probably quit in 3 days. But here I am."

She's now 12 journals deep.

Another friend opened his with:

"I've bought this overpriced notebook to vent about my overpriced therapist."

(A healthy self-awareness. And by the way — he's still journaling.)

Your first entry doesn't need to be noble. It can be:

- A rant
- A question
- A doodle
- A grocery list
- A sentence like "Wow, this pen writes well."

It's all allowed. Because you're not writing *for* the journal. You're writing *for* yourself.

💡 Tips to Ease Into the First Entry

Here are five ways to make your debut easier:

1. **Write as if no one will read it** — because no one has to. That's the beauty of journaling.
2. **Use a prompt** (like the ones at the end of this chapter).
3. **Begin with "Today I noticed…"** – a powerful gateway to awareness.
4. **Set a timer for 5 minutes** – write anything until the buzzer.
5. **Let your hand move faster than your inner critic.** You can't judge a sentence you didn't give time to judge.

📜 Why This Page Matters (Even If It Feels Small)

Your first entry is like your first walk after months of inactivity.

It might be clumsy. Short. Stiff.

But it's movement.

And movement turns into momentum.

No one writes a life-changing journal entry on day one. But the fact that you **began** — that's already a shift. That's already a change.

Imagine coming back to this first page 6 months from now. You'll smile. You'll see how far you've come. You'll remember the hesitation — and celebrate that you didn't let it win.

✐ Your First Entry Might Not Be Your Best

And that's the point.

It's the scratch on the record. The crack in the ice. The inhale before the real music starts.

The beauty of journaling is that **no entry defines you — but all of them reveal you**.

So don't aim for brilliance. Aim for honesty.

Don't worry about grammar. Worry about showing up.

Don't edit. Just express.

You're not writing a memoir.

You're opening a window.

And what comes through might surprise you.

📖 Prompt: Just One Page

Here's a starter you can use right now:

"What made me want to journal today?"

Or

"What do I wish someone understood about me right now?"

Write for just **one page**. That's all.

No more. No less.

Let the page meet you where you are.

☌ Final Thoughts

Don't turn your first entry into a ceremony.

Treat it like a conversation — awkward at first, honest in time, transformative if you stick with it.

If the page feels scary, that means it matters.

So take a deep breath. Write a word.

Then another.

Congratulations — you've started.

"A journey of a thousand miles begins with a single step."

— *Lao Tzu*

In your case, that step is about 15 lines long. On a slightly coffee-stained page. With a not-so-fancy pen. And the courage to begin.

Chapter Summary
Starting from Scratch

Starting a journaling practice is often the hardest part—not because we don't know it's good for us, but because getting past the first step can feel intimidating. This chapter gently walked you through that vulnerable threshold by breaking down the invisible blockers that hold so many people back.

We began by looking at **why starting is hard**—how overthinking, expectations, and perfectionism make us stall. You saw real-life stories that proved once you begin, momentum follows.

From there, we dove into **overcoming the blank page**, offering practical ways to begin writing even when you "have nothing to say." You learned how your first entry doesn't need to be poetic—it just needs to be *honest*. We even peeked into the first entries of journaling icons like Anne Frank and Marcus Aurelius to show that greatness often begins with modest words.

Next, we explored **choosing your tools**—notebooks, pens, apps, and journaling spaces. You discovered that the right tools can ease friction and make the practice inviting. Through humor and real stories (like the spilled coffee incident!), you were reminded: the best tools are the ones that make you *want* to come back.

Finally, we talked about **your first entry**—what to write, how to approach it without fear, and how to allow that first step to be small, imperfect, and freeing.

This chapter wasn't just about writing—it was about **permission**. Permission to be messy. To be new. To be honest. And most of all, to begin.

"You don't have to get it right. You just have to get it started."

— *Marie Forleo*

Your pen is ready.

Let's keep going.

🖊 Your Turn: From Small Steps to Five Honest Pages

You've already shown up for five days.

You wrote 3–5 lines each day — small but powerful check-ins. You cracked open the door to journaling and let a little bit of yourself onto the page.

That was your warm-up.

Now, let's stretch the practice a little more. No pressure. Just a little more space to breathe, reflect, and listen inward.

🎯 The "First Five Pages" Challenge

Here's your next workout:

Write five entries over the next seven days. Fill one page per entry.

Not a perfect page. Not a poetic page. Just **your** page.

Each entry can begin with a gentle nudge like:

🜂 **Entry 1** — "Right now, this is where I'm at…"

Start with honesty. What's going on in your world — internally or externally?

🔄 **Entry 2** — "A moment that shifted my mood recently…"

It could be a conversation, a text, a memory, or a feeling.

🌱 **Entry 3** — "Something I'm learning about myself…"

No need to be profound — just curious. Patterns, reactions, or surprises.

🔑 **Entry 4** — "If I could write a letter to my past self, it would say…"

Speak with kindness to who you once were.

🔥 **Entry 5** — "What I want more of — and what I want less of."

Clarity often lives in contrast.

💡 Tip: Don't worry if your handwriting is messy. Don't overthink your grammar. You're not crafting literature — you're cultivating self-awareness.

Some entries may feel clear. Others may feel foggy. That's okay. Keep the pen moving. Trust the page.

"Start where you are. Use what you have. Do what you can."

— *Arthur Ashe*

Chapter 3

Restarting After You Stop

The Hardest Step Serena Williams Ever Took

Before Serena Williams became a 23-time Grand Slam champion, she almost quit tennis.

It was 2011. She had won nearly everything there was to win. But a series of health scares—including a pulmonary embolism that nearly took her life—left her physically drained and emotionally fractured. For months, she didn't touch a racquet. No gym. No practice. Just long days of recovery and reflection. And doubt.

In an interview later, she admitted: *"I didn't think I could come back. I didn't know where to start. What if I'd lost the spark? What if I wasn't Serena anymore?"*

The pressure of returning to form—of becoming *herself* again—felt overwhelming.

So, she delayed.

Then one day, a friend suggested she just go hit a few balls. *"Just rally,"* they said. No drills. No coaches. No targets.

Reluctantly, she walked onto the court. Racket in hand. Familiar, but foreign.

The first few shots were clumsy. Her timing was off. Her footwork was slow. But as minutes passed, something clicked. Her body remembered. Her mind relaxed. The rhythm returned.

One hour turned into two.

She walked off the court drenched in sweat—and smiling.

That day didn't make headlines. No trophies, no glory. But in many ways, it was her greatest win. Because she started.

And that changed everything.

Within a year, Serena was back to winning Grand Slams. But more importantly, she often called that first comeback practice her most *mentally important* session ever. Not because it was impressive. But because it happened.

"The will to win is important, but the will to prepare is vital." – Joe Paterno

That first step? That's where most people stall. We think the mountain ahead is too steep. But often, it's not the climb—it's just the first step that feels heavy.

And when it comes to journaling, that heavy step looks like a fresh notebook, an unused pen... and a page that stares back at you.

You don't have to be great to start, but you have to start to be great." – Zig Ziglar

The Myth of Consistency: When I Tried to Be a Journaling Monk

And Why Missing Two Years Didn't Mean I Failed

Let me tell you the story of my most *delusional*, most *optimistic*, most *motivated* self.

Let's call him **"January Me."**

Every year, January Me shows up like a motivational speaker who's read seven books over New Year's weekend and seen two viral TED Talks. He has plans. Not goals — *systems*. He downloads four habit trackers, listens to atomic routines on 1.5x speed, and sets intentions that sound like they came from a mindfulness retreat brochure.

And of course — he buys *not one*, but **three new journals**.

One for goals.

One for gratitude.

One for dreams.

Because, obviously, each dimension of my personality deserves its own leather-bound sanctuary.

January Me wakes up early. January Me drinks warm lemon water with turmeric.

January Me sits cross-legged, lights a cinnamon-scented candle, and prepares to write deep, profound reflections like:

"What does the universe want from me today?"

"How might I dissolve resistance with presence?"

"Am I living from purpose or preference?"

It's beautiful.

Until it isn't.

By mid-January, **Real Me** shows up. The version with deadlines.

The version who forgets where he put his charger, misses two client calls, and accidentally reuses the same gym socks from last week.

One night, I forgot to journal.

The next day? I forgot again.

Then came the classic three-step descent:

1. **Guilt** ("You were doing so well…"),
2. **Avoidance** ("I'll catch up on Sunday — maybe do a 5-page entry?"), and
3. **Abandonment** ("It's already messed up. What's the point?")

And that *beautiful hardcover journal*? The one with the gold edges and motivational quote on the cover? It sat on my desk — judging me silently.

Eventually, I slid it under a stack of papers like an ex I wasn't ready to delete from my contacts.

Days turned into weeks. Weeks into months.

And then — I stopped journaling **altogether**.

Not for a week.

Not for a month.

But for **two full years**.

Yes, the "guy who journals daily" — the guy who had once *led workshops on reflective writing* — didn't write a single entry for over 700 days.

I told myself I was "too busy."

I told myself I'd "get back to it when things settled."

But the real reason?

I was afraid of the **shame** I might see on the page.

What would I even write?

"Hi again. Sorry. It's been 729 days. I hope you weren't waiting."

And then, during a particularly overwhelming week — no dramatic crisis, just general life fatigue — I found myself reaching for a pen.

Out of nowhere.

I pulled open the drawer, dusted off *that same journal*, flipped past the untouched pages, and wrote:

"Okay, so I messed up. But I'm here. Can we pick up where we left off?"

I didn't write a long reflection. I didn't recap two years. I didn't even date the entry properly.

But that moment? It felt like **coming home**!

🫧 Why We Crave Consistency (and Fear Interruptions)

There's something seductive about the idea of being "on a streak." It gives us a sense of momentum, of building something. Apps love it. People post about it. "120-day meditation streak!" or "Logged 90 days of gratitude journaling!"

It's motivating... until it isn't.

The moment we miss a day, the shame spiral begins. Suddenly, the 30 days of progress mean *nothing* — because we missed one. We feel like we've broken a sacred rule.

But here's the truth no one prints on planners:

Consistency is not about never stopping. It's about always returning.

Even the greatest athletes miss workouts. Writers skip writing. Spiritual teachers skip meditation. It's part of being human.

🎯 For the Reader: Let Go of the Pressure

So if you've ever skipped a day — or a week — or an entire year...

Please know this:

- You are not behind.
- You are not broken.
- You haven't ruined anything.

You are human. And being human means forgetting and returning. Wandering and remembering.

The pages are always there — not to punish, but to welcome.

From "Trying to Be Consistent" to "Why We Quit"

So much of the journaling struggle isn't about the **act** of writing — it's about the **expectation** to do it perfectly.

Once we drop the myth that we need to be consistent to be successful, a new question arises:

If we don't have to be perfect, then why do we still stop?

Why do so many of us fall off — even after we've experienced the benefits?

Why do blank pages become harder to face the longer we stay away?

In the next section, let's take an honest look at what really gets in the way. Because it's rarely laziness. It's often something softer, quieter... and far more human.

Let's explore that.

Why We Stop: The Case of the Vanishing Journals

Let's face it — we've all been there. That fresh notebook, that new pen, that surge of motivation. We tell ourselves, *"This time, I'm going to be consistent."*

And then... we stop.

But why?

Why do we stop journaling when we know it's good for us?

Let me share a few stories — some mine, some from others, all painfully, hilariously human.

✥ 1. The Perfection Trap

A friend of mine, bought a leather-bound journal from Italy. He spent ₹3,200 on it, because, in his words, *"If I buy something fancy, I'll definitely stick to it."*

His first entry was a masterstroke — calligraphy-level handwriting, a quote by Rumi, and perfectly structured reflections.

Day 2: He wrote a haiku *(a short Japanese-style poem with a 5-7-5 syllable pattern, often used to capture a moment or feeling). It read:*

Blank page in my hand

Thoughts are hiding from my pen

Maybe snacks will help

Day 3: He didn't write at all because, as he said, *"I wasn't feeling poetic enough."*

Day 5: He said, *"This journal deserves better than my random thoughts."*

Day 7: The journal quietly joined the stack of "aspirational objects" — right next to the unopened yoga mat.

We stop because we believe our words have to be Instagram-worthy. That journaling has to sound wise. But let's remember — your journal is not your CV. It's not an art gallery. It's a sandbox. Messy is welcome.

🧠 2. The Overwhelm Spiral

Then there's the classic case of "I'll write when I have time."

This was me — in my early days, trying to journal like I was writing a novel. Each entry had to cover *everything* — childhood trauma, existential dread, dreams, to-do lists, grocery items, and reflections on the meaning of time.

The result? I avoided writing for days.

Why? Because each time I thought of journaling, I imagined having to summarize the last 96 hours of life. I called it *"catch-up paralysis."*

Eventually, I realized: You don't need to write *everything*. You just need to write *something*.

A single thought. A sentence. Even "today sucked."

That counts.

🧑 💼 3. The "Busy" Badge

Let's be honest — one of the most common reasons we stop?

"I don't have time."

It sounds valid. But here's what I discovered: during one of my busiest weeks — 14 meetings, two deadlines, and one broken washing machine — I managed to scroll social media for 4.5 hours (my phone reminded me, not out of kindness, but shame).

We have time. We just don't prioritize silence.

Because sometimes, silence can be scarier than noise.

We say we're too busy, but what we really mean is: *"I'm afraid to sit with myself."* And that's okay. But let's call it what it is.

📈 4. The Emotional Rollercoaster

Another reason we stop journaling? We only show up when we're either floating or falling.

When things are amazing, we say, *"I'm too happy to write."*

When things are rough, we say, *"I don't want to think about it right now."*

We skip journaling because we think we need to be in the *right mood* for it.

But journaling isn't a spa treatment. It's more like brushing your teeth. Some days are minty fresh. Some days, you just show up and scrub. You don't need to be in the mood — you just need to be present.

😂 5. The Guilty Comeback

Let me tell you about the time I journaled after a two-year gap.

I picked up my old journal and saw the last entry was from December 2019. I flipped the page and started writing:

"Dear Journal,

Wow. Sorry for ghosting you. A LOT has happened. Pandemic. Lockdowns. Banana bread. Existential dread. A haircut I regret.

But hey, I'm back."

That was it.

That entry made me laugh — and it reminded me why I write in the first place: not to be impressive, but to be real.

We stop because we believe we've "failed" the habit. But truth is, the only failure is *never* coming back.

🎙 6. Famous People Stop Too

Even legends hit pause.

Did you know Oprah Winfrey, who often speaks about gratitude journaling, admitted she stopped writing for almost a year?

In her own words:

"I got caught up in the doing, in the busyness of life, and thought I was too tired to write. Then one day I realized I wasn't too tired — I was too disconnected from myself."

She picked up her journal again, not to chase consistency, but to chase connection.

That's the magic: you don't need 365 perfect entries. You just need to keep returning.

💡 *So... Why Do We Stop?*

Because we're human.

Because life happens.

Because we expect perfection.

Because we don't want to face certain emotions.

Because we forget how small the act really is.

But stopping doesn't mean failing.

Stopping is part of the rhythm. And journaling, at its best, is not about streaks — it's about return.

✍ *If You've Stopped…*

If you've abandoned a journal, start a new page and write this:

"Hello again."

No explanations. No guilt. No justifications.

That line alone is brave. That line alone is a victory.

📌 *Call to Action:*

Take out your old journal or open a new notebook. Write today's date. Then write one sentence:

"I'm showing up again."

That's it. That's your restart.

🎯 *Final Thought*

You don't have to be perfect.

You don't have to be daily.

You just have to be willing.

As the brilliant author Anne Lamott once said:

"Almost everything will work again if you unplug it for a few minutes… including you."

Your journal is the socket.

Go plug in.

3. The Guilt Loop: Why Missing One Day Feels Like Failing a Lifetime

Let's talk about guilt — that sly inner narrator who shows up whenever we *don't* do what we said we would.

You miss a day of journaling, and suddenly you're not just someone who skipped writing. No. You're a person who *never finishes anything,* who lacks discipline, who is probably disappointing your future self and the spirit of Anne Frank simultaneously.

Too much? Probably. But that's what guilt does — it exaggerates.

And if you've ever felt too guilty to return to journaling, this chapter is for you.

Guilt is Not the Villain. The Loop Is.

It's not guilt alone that derails us — it's what guilt turns into when left unchecked: **The Guilt Loop**.

Here's how it works:

1. You miss a day.
2. You feel bad about it.
3. You avoid journaling because you feel bad.
4. More time passes. Guilt grows.
5. Now you're not just avoiding the act of writing — you're avoiding the *feeling* of having not written.

6. Repeat from step 2.

Before you know it, two weeks have passed, the notebook looks like a stranger, and starting again feels like walking back into a party where you ghosted the host.

Real-Life Example: My "Forgive Me, Journal" Entry

I once skipped journaling for three whole months. Life got busy, may be. But mostly, I felt... off. I didn't know how to pick it back up again.

When I finally opened the journal, the last entry was this beautiful, hopeful goal-setting vision board for the "best year of my life."

I felt like a fraud.

I stared at the empty page for a long time. And then I wrote:

"Okay... it's been a while. I don't really know why I stopped. But I'm here now. Let's just start from today."

And just like that — the guilt eased. Not because I'd made up for lost time. But because I gave myself permission to be real. I allowed honesty to replace perfection.

But full confession: on another comeback attempt, I went full drama. That entry read:

"Dear Journal,

I know it's been 73 days. Please don't slam the cover on me. I got distracted by email, YouTube, and emotional overeating. But I've returned. With a pen. And snacks. Let's never speak of this again."

That one made me laugh out loud. And sometimes, that's all it takes — a little self-forgiveness with a side of humor.

Because the moment you write anything — even a silly confession — you're back. The loop is broken. The pen is moving. You're in.

The Oprah Excuse I Didn't Know I Needed

Later, I found comfort in learning that even Oprah Winfrey — the Queen of Talk Shows and the woman who practically turned gratitude into a global movement — once admitted she fell off the journaling wagon when life got too hectic. Her famously consistent habit of recording daily gratitudes began to slip as her schedule became more demanding.

If Oprah could pause her sacred ritual while building a media empire, maybe I could forgive myself for skipping journaling during my own intense season of... watching productivity hacks on YouTube. (While being impressively unproductive.)

I mean, she ruled daytime television for 25 years — I can't even rule my own remote.

If Oprah could pick up the pen again with grace, surely I could return after months of aimless screen time, bingeing the same "How Ancient Egyptians Baked Bread" documentary on loop, and watching reels of "Cat Fight Dog."

That's the real win — not perfection, but the honest return. Preferably with snacks, a sense of humor, and zero pressure to be profound.

4. The Gentle Re-entry

Because You're Not a Robot... and That's Okay

So, you fell off the journaling wagon. You missed a few days... or a few weeks... or let's be honest, you haven't touched your journal since that New Year's resolution you wrote with great optimism in a new pen that cost more than your monthly phone bill.

It's fine. Really.

Because here's the truth no one tells you in those glossy self-help books with soft-lit covers: **falling off is not failure.** It's just... life.

Let's take a moment to appreciate that even Google Docs autosaves your half-finished thoughts. You, too, are allowed to pick up where you left off.

📁 Re-entry Tool #1: The "No Context Comeback"

You don't need a long explanation. You don't need to justify your absence. You can literally just write:

"Hi again, notebook."

"Oops."

"Where were we?"

Or, my personal favorite:

"Insert dramatic re-entrance music here."

The journal doesn't judge. It's not your boss. It doesn't need reasons. It just needs your honesty.

🧠 Re-entry Tool #2: Use a Prompt

Feeling awkward? Start with something neutral. These prompts are like journal icebreakers:

- "What have I been thinking about a lot lately?"
- "What's one thing that's been quietly bothering me?"
- "What's something I haven't said out loud — even to myself?"

If those feel too deep, try these:

- "What's the weirdest thing I Googled this week?"
- "If my mood was a weather report, what would it be?"
- "What would my cat/dog/houseplant/anything say about my week?"

✍️ Re-entry Tool #3: Doodle or List

Words failing you? That's okay. Make a list. Sketch a mood. Scribble something completely unrelated — like potential superhero names for yourself (mine was "Captain Overthinker").

You're not writing for Pulitzer. You're writing for **presence**.

The Guilt-Free Formula for Re-Entry:

1. **Open the journal.**
2. **Write anything.**
3. **Close the journal (optional).**
4. **Repeat tomorrow.**

🎤 *A Word from the Famous:*

Author Elizabeth Gilbert, in one interview, shared that her journaling is often messy, boring, and rambling. Some entries are just to-do lists. Others are confessions. Some are shopping lists pretending to be spiritual reflections. And that's okay.

Her words?

"Just show up. That's the discipline. The magic comes later."

One More Real-Life Comeback Entry

Here's what i once wrote after a 5-month break:

"Dear Journal, I don't know what day it is. I don't know what I'm doing. But I missed you. Let's pretend I never left."

That entry led to one of the most insightful weeks of writing I've ever had. Not because I planned it. But because I **allowed it**.

Remember:

This isn't about catching up.

It's about showing up.

So, dust off the journal. Crack that stiff spine open. And re-enter not with fireworks — but with forgiveness.

And maybe a cookie

5. Making Peace with the Gaps

Because Life Happens, and That's the Point

You know those sleek journals on Instagram? The ones with color-coded entries, floral stickers, mood tracker charts, and daily affirmations in calligraphy?

Yeah. Mine doesn't look like that either.

Mine looks like:

- Three pages of deep reflections
- A sketch of a coffee mug
- Two torn pages where I attempted poetry
- ...and then, a six-month silence followed by a single line:

"Welp."

The truth is, **gaps happen**. You stop. Life throws things at you. Or you just... drift. It's not failure. It's just being human.

✴ *Real-Life Example: My "Gap Year"*

There was a time I didn't journal for an entire year. Not one word. No reason, really. Just work stress, Netflix, deadlines, social media rabbit holes, and an unfortunate obsession with watching videos of people power-washing sidewalks.

Then, one Sunday afternoon, I opened my old journal — dusty, judgy, dramatic. The last entry read:

"This year, I will write every day. No excuses."

Well... that aged beautifully.

But instead of feeling ashamed, I laughed. Then I picked up my pen and wrote:

"Let's pretend that year was just an unusually long breath."

That line became my peace treaty.

🧘 ♀ *Reframe the Gaps: They're Part of the Practice*

You don't apologize to your dumbbells for skipping the gym. You don't apologize to your plants for forgetting to water them (okay, maybe you do... but they're dramatic). So why apologize to your journal?

Gaps aren't signs of failure. They're signs of life.

Think of journaling like breathing — sometimes deep and regular, sometimes quick and irregular. And sometimes, you hold your breath without realizing.

That's okay.

The important thing is: **you come back.**

✍ Write Your Gap a Love Letter

Here's a quirky exercise you can try:

Write a love letter to your gap.

"Dear 84-Day Silence,

Thank you for reminding me that I don't need to be perfect to return. You gave me space to miss this practice. You let me live a bit — and now I'm ready to make sense of it."

That letter may make you smile. And that smile may give the momentum to write again the next day. (And again the day after that. And then... okay, then you forgot again. But still.)

⬤ The Donut Theory

Think of journaling like a donut.

Yes, it's round. Yes, it's comforting. But most importantly — it has a hole.

That gap in the middle? That's part of what makes it a donut. That's its shape. Without it, it would just be a strange, dense roll.

Likewise, your journal is not ruined by gaps — it's **defined** by them. They make the full picture honest. Real. Relatable.

🗣 Even the Pros Miss Days

Did you know that *Austin Kleon*, author of *Steal Like an Artist*, once tweeted that half his journal is just him apologizing to his journal for not writing?

It happens to everyone — artists, writers, CEOs, Oprah (yep, even her — we covered that already).

So, What Now?

- **Open the journal.** No dramatic re-entry. Just… hello again.
- **Write the date.** That alone is enough.
- **Write one line.** "I'm back." "Life's been a blur." "I had biryani today."
- **And smile.** Because gaps don't mean you're broken. They mean you're living.

💬 Parting Line:

"The pages you didn't write still count — because they're part of the story that brought you back."

— Probably Not Socrates, but Let's Go With It

6. Rituals of Renewal

Because Sometimes, You Need to Light a Candle... or Just Find Your Favorite Pen Again.

Let's face it: restarting anything — whether it's exercise, meditation, or journaling — is rarely graceful. It's more like trying to jump onto a moving train... in pajamas... holding a coffee.

That's where **rituals of renewal** come in. They're not about perfection. They're not about productivity. They're about *permission* — to begin again, gently, intentionally, and without guilt.

◈ *Why Rituals Work*

Human beings love **symbolic fresh starts** — New Year's Day, birthdays, Mondays (even if we pretend to hate them). It's why we cut our hair after a breakup. Or reorganize the fridge when life feels messy.

Rituals signal to the brain: *"Hey, we're turning the page now."*

They mark the moment. They help us arrive.

And journaling is no different.

♀ **Real-Life Example: The Candle That Wasn't Magic (But Almost)**

A friend of mine — let's call her Anjali — had fallen off her journaling habit for almost a year. One rainy afternoon, she decided she wanted to restart. But instead of rushing to write, she lit a candle. A small, lavender one.

Then she made chai. Sat near her window. Took five deep breaths. And only then, did she open her notebook.

Her first entry wasn't profound. It just said:

"I'm here. It's raining. My pen feels nervous. But I'm here."

That's it. But the **ritual** helped her arrive. The candle wasn't magic. But the *intention* was.

She's been journaling almost every week since.

Your Ritual Can Be Silly. That's the Point.

You don't have to light incense or chant Sanskrit verses (unless that's your vibe — in which case, namaste).

Your ritual could be:

- A playlist called "Dear Diary"
- Brewing a cup of your favourite tea
- Wearing your journaling socks (yes, that's a thing now)
- Scribbling a doodle before you write
- Telling your journal, "Brace yourself, it's about to get messy"

The goal isn't to impress your future biographers. It's to send a gentle cue to your brain: *"We're stepping into a sacred little corner now — just for us."*

🎯 Try This: A Ritual Menu

Pick one from each category to build your own ritual.

🕰 Timing

- Mornings before the noise begins
- Evenings with a warm drink
- Sundays as a weekly recap

📍 Space

- A cozy corner with a cushion
- Your parked car (surprisingly underrated)
- A random cafe where you pretend to be a poet

🛠 Tools

- A pen that feels like it "gets" you
- A notebook you like touching
- A candle, timer, playlist, or calming scent

💬 Mantra (Optional)

- "I'm here."
- "Let's see what shows up."
- "This is my truth corner."

🧘 📷 Ritual ≠ Routine

Let's be clear — this isn't about rigid routines or turning your journaling into a productivity hack.

This is about *ceremony without pressure.*

Because sometimes, lighting a candle is easier than untangling your thoughts. Sometimes, choosing the "right" pen is your warm-up. And sometimes, your ritual is just *showing up with bad handwriting and an open heart.*

✦ Famous People and Their Rituals

- **Maya Angelou** rented a hotel room just for writing — with nothing in it but a Bible, a bottle of sherry, and a yellow legal pad.

- **Joan Didion** kept her journal beside her bed and always wrote before dinner.

- **Steven Spielberg** sketches storyboards by hand to think through scenes — his ritual for unlocking creativity.

You don't need a hotel room. You just need **a moment that feels like a beginning.**

📝 Final Thought:

"It's not the candle or the cup of tea that changes you — it's the pause. The decision to begin again, gently."

— Rajiv Krishnan Pisharoti

7. Comeback Stories from the Page — Fresh Real-Life Examples

Emma Watson: The Reflective Actress

Who: British actress and activist known for playing Hermione Granger in the *Harry Potter* series.

Story: Emma Watson has openly spoken about her habit of journaling — not just for self-reflection but as a method to manage fame and anxiety. In interviews with *British Vogue* and on mental health panels, she revealed that at one point, the pace of her work and global attention overwhelmed her.

Her journaling habit—once steady—took a hit. She found herself too "emotionally exhausted to write".

But it was during her time off from acting post-*Beauty and the Beast* that she returned to it. Emma described journaling as "the way I talk to my truest self when the world is too noisy." She now claims to have filled over 30 journals, often scribbling thoughts at airports or between shoots. Her return to journaling was not perfect — it was staggered, messy, and occasional. But it was also healing.

Matthew McConaughey: The Greenlights Journals

Who: Oscar-winning actor and author of *Greenlights*

Story: Matthew McConaughey famously revealed that he'd been journaling since he was 14. However, in his mid-30s, as fame and success surged, he admits he "forgot to check in with himself." His journals collected dust while life moved fast.

Years later, in a hotel in the desert, he decided to gather those dusty journals and begin again. What followed was the writing of *Greenlights* — a bestselling memoir rooted in old entries, forgotten reflections, and rediscovered wisdom.

In his words: "I found stories I didn't remember living. Lessons I forgot I learned." That reconnection with the past sparked a creative revival and personal recalibration.

J.K. Rowling: Post-Success Reflection

Who: Author of the *Harry Potter* series.

Story: Rowling is known for writing on café napkins, but she's also a fierce advocate for introspection. After the release of her final *Harry Potter* book, she revealed in interviews that she fell into a kind of creative void. "For years, I wrote obsessively — and then I didn't know how to write without pressure."

During this pause, she returned to journaling not as an author, but as a woman figuring out life after global success. In 2008, during a Harvard commencement speech, she reflected on this period of uncertainty and used journaling to explore questions of purpose and reinvention.

Kevin Hart: From Breakdown to Breakthrough

Who: Comedian, actor, and entrepreneur.

Story: In 2019, Kevin Hart was involved in a near-fatal car accident. During his long rehabilitation, he admitted to struggling mentally and emotionally. A therapist suggested journaling.

Hart admitted he wasn't a "writing kind of guy" — but he tried it anyway. Over time, the notebook became his therapist, coach, and mirror. He wrote through the pain, the fear, and even the guilt of slowing down.

In interviews on *The Joe Rogan Experience* and *The School of Greatness* podcast, he credits journaling as one of the tools that helped him reframe his mindset and rebuild from the inside out.

Chapter Summary:
Restarting After You Stop

"Your journaling journey is not broken. It's just paused."

Life happens. Blank pages pile up. Weeks or even months pass. And then comes the guilt, the hesitation, the story we tell ourselves — "I've failed." But this chapter reminded us: **the act of returning is the true triumph.**

You explored how even the most successful people — from Serena Williams to Oprah Winfrey — have paused and restarted. You laughed through the myth of consistency (hello, January Me), saw how guilt loops trick us into shame, and discovered tools for a gentle re-entry.

Whether you've been away for 3 days or 3 years, your journal is still there. Unchanged. Patient. Ready.

And that's what this chapter was really about:

Journaling doesn't need perfection. It needs permission.

So take the pressure off. You don't need to catch up or be profound.

Just **start again** — with a smile, a snack, and maybe a fresh page.

From Restart to Routine: Where the Real Magic Happens

You've done the hard part — you've begun again. You've faced the guilt, acknowledged the gaps, and picked up the pen.

But here's where most of us trip up: we confuse a restart with a rhythm.

Restarting is like going on one great jog and calling yourself a marathoner. It feels good, it counts — but for real change, you need repetition. You need flow. You need a routine that doesn't feel like a punishment, but like brushing your teeth — no drama, just done.

And that's what this next chapter is about: turning the quiet act of journaling into a rhythm that feels natural, do-able, and even... something you miss when it's not there. Welcome to Chapter 4: The Mechanics of a Journaling Routine

Call to Action:

Pause. Breathe. Forgive the gap.
Now—turn the page.

Not because you *have* to, but because you *get* to.
Not to be perfect, but to be present.
Your journal is waiting, not for your best day, just your honest one.

So grab your pen, pour your favorite drink, and begin again.
One word is enough.
You've already restarted—now, let's make it a rhythm.

Chapter 4

The Mechanics of a Journaling Routine

Time of Day

Morning Musings or Midnight Rants? Finding Your Moment

Let's face it — you're not going to suddenly become a 5 AM sunrise gratitude whisperer if you've spent the last decade hitting snooze like it's a professional sport.

Some people swear by morning journaling. Others are night owls, processing their day in the moonlight. And some write at 3 PM, mid-meeting, while pretending to take notes (yes, I see you).

Real-Life Example: Ali Abdaal

Author and YouTuber **Ali Abdaal**, who juggles medical training and a massive online presence, journals at night. For him, it's like clearing mental tabs: what worked, what didn't, what's worth keeping. He says, "My brain wakes up when the world sleeps." And no, he doesn't light incense or wear a velvet robe while doing it. (Probably.)

When I Tried Morning Journaling...

Once, I tried morning journaling. I set the stage like a wellness influencer: candle lit, tea brewed, silence perfected. I even opened the curtains to let the sun bless my thoughts. Five minutes later? Face down on the table. Pen in hand. Tea cold. A tragic nap in cursive.

What the Research Says

According to multiple psychology studies, journaling at night may help people process emotions better, especially when reflecting on daily events. But journaling in the morning can reduce stress by helping plan and prioritize.

So what gives?

Your Energy, Your Choice

Some people are reflective at dawn. Others only find clarity when the dishes are done and the house is silent. Some get a second wind at 10 PM (we see you, existential overthinkers).

Journaling isn't about what looks good on a productivity blog. It's about what works for you.

The Goldilocks Principle of Timing

Not too early. Not too late. Just... right. Your "just right" might be:

- While the coffee brews
- On your commute (not while driving, please)
- During lunch breaks
- Right before bed

My Favorite Excuse (That Backfired)

I once told myself I was "too mentally foggy" to write in the morning. Then I spent 20 minutes composing the perfect passive-aggressive email to a colleague. So, turns out, I *could* string sentences together. Just needed the right motivation.

Key Tip:

Pick a time that matches your real-life rhythm, not your aspirational Pinterest board. Don't force sunrise meditations if your brain hits snooze. Don't try midnight journaling if you turn into a confused potato after 9 PM.

In Summary:

- There's no perfect time — there's just *your* time.
- Morning, noon, or night — they all work.
- Don't wait for the vibe. Create a small window. Make it yours.
- You don't need a halo of enlightenment — just five minutes and a pen.

Let's move on to choosing the tools that'll actually make you want to come back

Subtopic 2: Digital vs. Analog

The Pen or the Pixel? The Eternal Showdown

Let's start with the age-old question:

"Should I journal by hand or on a screen?"

It's right up there with other modern dilemmas like:

- "Should I reply to this message now or ghost them forever?"
- "Is this a headache or am I dying?"

Okay, maybe not that dramatic. But the journaling debate is real.

📝 *Team Analog: Lovers of Paper and Pen*

These are the folks who swear there's magic in ink. They say the scratch of a pen is therapeutic. That the smell of fresh paper boosts creativity. That they can't *really* think unless they're writing by hand.

And you know what? They're not wrong.

Jack Dorsey, co-founder of Twitter and Square, journals by hand. Despite building two of the most digital-forward platforms in the world, he prefers paper. Why? He says it slows him down. Helps him think more clearly. No distractions. No notifications. No pop-ups suggesting you buy a blender mid-thought.

For many, handwriting is like mindful movement. The brain slows down. Ideas settle. And bonus: no one can read your entries — including you.

✦ Bonus Tip:

If privacy is your concern, handwriting in near-illegible cursive is an underrated encryption method.

💻 *Team Digital: Tap, Type, Don't Look Back*

On the flip side are the digital die-hards — people who say, "If I can't Ctrl+Z it, I don't trust it." Their journals live in apps, cloud folders, and encrypted vaults. They love being able to search entries, tag emotions, add emojis, and never worry about running out of pages.

These are the people who type faster than they think. For them, journaling is part brain-dump, part tech workout.

Real-Life Example: Author and entrepreneur **Tim Ferriss** has talked about using a mix of handwritten and digital tools. He starts his day with a physical journal (his "morning pages"), but then moves insights or ideas into digital notes so he can search and reflect later. It's like journaling with one foot in the forest, and one foot in Silicon Valley.

Personal Confession:

I once downloaded a journaling app that let me tag my feelings with emojis.

My entry looked like this:

"Today I feel: 😩 ☕ 🐮 🙉 🍪."

Translation? I was tired, caffeinated, overwhelmed, melting emotionally, and really needed a cookie.

💡 *The Pros and Cons Showdown*

Feature	Analog (Paper)	Digital (App/Laptop)
Sensory Pleasure	Pen! Ink! Satisfying scratch	Glowing screen + blue light
Search Function	Flip, flip, flip	Just type a word—voilà!
Privacy	Hide under bed	Password-protected cloud
Backup	Lost journal = heartbreak	Auto-sync = peace of mind
Distraction Level	Low (unless paper flies off)	High (hello Instagram tab)
Aesthetic Vibes	Moody candle shots on Insta	Spreadsheet chic?

🥊 📷 *So... Which One's Better?*

Here's the truth: **Neither. And both.**

It's not about what looks cooler on your desk. It's about **what you'll actually use.**

The best journaling method is the one that makes it easier for you to return. Not once. But often.

Do you like the feel of a pen in your hand? Go for a physical notebook.

Can't stand your handwriting and love organizing thoughts by tags? Digital it is.

Want the best of both worlds? Start on paper. Snap a photo. Upload it. Boom — hybrid model.

Real-Life Hack:

One of my friends writes quick notes during her commute using a voice-to-text journaling app. It's chaotic, full of typos, and sometimes misinterprets what she says, but it's real. She once told the app, "I'm feeling hopeful today," and it wrote "I'm feeding a hopeful donkey." And honestly? Still therapeutic.

🧠 *Final Thought:*

You're not trying to win a journaling Oscar here. There's no "Best Medium" award. Just pick the tool that feels easy, natural, and non-threatening.

If journaling feels like a chore, you won't do it. But if it feels like a break — a breather — a private check-in — you'll come back. Again and again.

🎯 *Tip to Try:*

Test both. Write for a week in a notebook. Then try digital for a week. Compare how you feel. Your ideal method may surprise you.

✍️ *Closing Line:*

Whether you journal in a Moleskine or a Google Doc, on handmade paper or an app that reminds you with emojis, the point is not the container. It's the connection.

So pen or pixel — just start writing.

Subtopic 3: Time Anchors

Hook It to a Habit

You don't need more time. You need better anchors.

We often think that journaling requires a special pocket of time — a perfect sunrise, a quiet house, a cup of herbal tea in hand. But let's be honest: if you're waiting for the perfect moment, you might be waiting until retirement.

That's where **time anchors** come in. Time anchors are everyday habits that are already baked into your schedule — things you do so regularly, you don't even think about them anymore. These are the perfect moments to *hook* a new habit onto.

Because habits, like friendships, are more likely to stick if they come with a ride.

What's a time anchor?

A time anchor is any consistent action or routine you already do. Think:

- Brushing your teeth
- Brewing your first cup of coffee
- Waiting for your computer to boot up
- Sitting in the car during your child's piano class
- Standing in line for your daily overpriced smoothie

The key is to **tie journaling to something that already happens — reliably — in your day**. That way, your brain starts associating one habit with the other.

For example:

- "I journal right after I brush my teeth."
- "I write 3 lines while my toast is toasting."
- "I jot a thought down while waiting for my dog to finish sniffing every tree on the block."

It doesn't have to be dramatic. It just has to be regular.

Real-Life Example: Hasan Minhaj and the Subway Journaling

Comedian and political storyteller **Hasan Minhaj** shared in an interview that during his early years in New York, he would use his subway commute to reflect. It wasn't quiet. It wasn't elegant. It was him, a notebook, and the Q train.

He didn't wait for inspiration to strike. He used what he had — a moving train, ten minutes of downtime, and the thoughts bouncing around in his head.

Sometimes he wrote jokes. Sometimes questions.

But the point is — **he anchored his journaling to a moment already in his day.**

No desk. No candle. Just presence.

Humorous Side Note:

I tried journaling before my morning run. Only problem? I don't run. Ever.

Moral of the story: don't anchor a habit to a fantasy. Anchor it to reality.

Other Funny (and "may be" Real) Anchor Moments:

- A friend journals on the toilet. He says, "It's the only place I'm left alone." Respect.

- Another scribbles in her notebook while waiting for the microwave to beep. She calls it "one-minute mindfulness."

- Someone once journaled in the Uber pool with someone snoring next to him. The entry was mostly about his snore pattern. Still counts.

Why Anchoring Works

According to behavioural psychology, new habits are more likely to stick when they're paired with existing ones. This technique, known as **habit stacking**, was popularized by James Clear in his book *Atomic Habits.*

His formula? "After [current habit], I will [new habit]."

It's genius because you're not creating time — you're repurposing it.

So instead of saying:

"I'll journal sometime today" (which usually turns into "tomorrow"), you say:

"After I sip my coffee, I'll write 3 lines."

You've got coffee every day. Now your journal does, too.

Common Anchors to Consider:

- After breakfast
- Before checking social media

- After reading a page from a book
- While waiting for Zoom calls to begin
- Right before bed

And remember: anchors don't need to be beautiful. They need to be **consistent.**

A Journal Entry Doesn't Need a Candle

We often romanticize journaling.

We imagine a gorgeous desk, incense burning, perfectly sharpened pencils, and music beats in the background.

But real journaling happens:

- In between toddler tantrums
- While eating cereal
- In parked cars
- On the backs of receipts

The trick isn't to make journaling beautiful. It's to make it *happen.*

Even one line.

Your Turn: Find Your Anchor

Take a moment. Think of two things you already do every day — without fail. That's your anchor.

Now try this:

"After I __________, I will journal for 2 minutes."

Just 2 minutes. That's perhaps shorter than most reels.

Try it for 3 days in a row.

No judgment. No pressure.

Just you, your anchor, and your page.

The goal isn't a perfect record. The goal is to make the act of writing feel like coming up for air.

Hook your journal to your life. It'll hold.

Subtopic 4: Space and Place

Title: Your Journaling Nook Doesn't Need a Himalayan Salt Lamp

While you don't need a candlelit writing cave, having a consistent space makes a difference.

Examples of spaces that work:

- Your bedside table
- A corner of the kitchen counter
- A random bench in your office lobby (true story)

Real-Life Example: Actor **Tom Hanks** reportedly writes and journals in hotel rooms, using them as temporary sanctuaries. "I unpack my thoughts before I unpack my bags," he joked.

A Confession: A journaling space? The bathroom. Because it's the only room in my house where people don't interrupt me. Usually.

Tip: Designate a space that says, "This is your time." It doesn't have to be pretty. It has to be *yours*.

Subtopic 5: Rituals Before Writing

Title: The Cue, the Crutch, and the Coffee

We are ritualistic creatures. Even if our "ritual" is just dramatically sighing before we do something important.

Ideas for simple journaling rituals:

- Light a candle
- Play a specific playlist
- Sip a particular tea
- Open to a bookmarked quote

Real-Life Example: Novelist **Haruki Murakami** follows strict writing rituals — including waking at 4 AM, running, and listening to jazz. That sounds excessive for journaling. But even he says the *ritual* is what keeps the writing sacred.

Humorous Add-On: My ritual? Whispering to my pen: "Please don't make me cry today."

Key Takeaway: A simple ritual can tell your brain: "It's time to tune in." Not scroll. Not scroll *again*. But *write*.

Chapter Summary:
Routines That Don't Require Superpowers

The main message is that routines don't have to be strict or demanding — they simply need to be sustainable and suited to your real life. Instead of chasing an idealized version of productivity, find a time of day that fits naturally into your actual schedule. Morning pages may work for some, while others may find quiet moments in the evening more realistic. The key is to make journaling a part of life as it is, not how you wish it were.

The chapter also stresses the importance of using tools you genuinely enjoy. Whether you prefer the feel of pen on paper or the convenience of typing on a phone or laptop, the best tools are the ones you'll actually stick with. There's no need for fancy journals or perfect pens — just choose what makes the process inviting.

A powerful strategy discussed is to anchor journaling to an existing habit. This could be pairing it with your morning coffee, after brushing your teeth, or just before bed. Doing so builds consistency effortlessly. Creating a small, dedicated space for journaling — even just a corner of a desk — can also help signal that it's time to write.

Finally, the author recommends developing a simple ritual that tells your brain it's journaling time. This could be lighting a candle, playing soft music, or taking a deep breath. These small actions prime your mind for reflection and expression.

Overall, this chapter reminds us that journaling routines aren't about discipline or perfection. They're about creating conditions that make it easier to show up — calmly, consistently, and without pressure.

Call to Action – Chapter 4: Build Your "Real-Life" Routine

Now that you understand *why* journaling matters and how to quiet the inner critic or overcome resistance , it's time to take the next gentle step: create a journaling routine that fits *your* life — not someone else's idea of the "perfect" routine.

Don't wait for a magical burst of motivation or the ideal conditions. Instead:

- **Pick a time** that genuinely works with your current schedule — even 5 minutes counts.
- **Choose a tool** you enjoy using, whether that's your favorite pen, a journaling app, or sticky notes.
- **Anchor journaling** to something you already do every day — like coffee, commuting, or bedtime.
- **Set up a small, inviting space**, even if it's just your kitchen table for five minutes.
- **Create a ritual** that helps your brain shift into "journaling mode" — a breath, a stretch, or a candle.

Start small. Start real. And most importantly, start *now*.

You don't need superpowers — you just need to show up as you are.

In Chapter 4, we created a journaling *routine* that fits real life. Now, in Chapter 5, we'll take that routine and turn it into an *effortless habit*. Because when you build a habit, you don't need motivation — just a cup of coffee and muscle memory.

Chapter 5

Making it a Habit

The Myth of Willpower

(Or why you're not lazy, just a human with Netflix and snacks)

Let's bust a myth right now: **willpower is not a reliable strategy** for doing anything consistently — especially not journaling. If willpower were enough, we'd all wake up at 5 a.m., run a 10K, write 500 words of soul-searching brilliance, and still have time to bake the finest bread before work.

Spoiler: that's not what happens.

What actually happens? You *intend* to journal. You really do. You even tell yourself, "After dinner, I'm going to write for 10 minutes." But then dinner becomes dessert, dessert becomes Instagram, and suddenly you're watching a documentary about competitive rock balancing while thinking, "I should write that down," and then... you don't.

Why? Because **willpower is like your phone battery at 1%** — unreliable, short-lived, and prone to shutting down just when you need it.

🧠 Your Brain is Not Lazy — It's Efficient (Read: Sneaky)

Willpower relies on your prefrontal cortex — the brain's CEO. But your CEO gets tired. It's been making decisions all day — answering emails, resisting the urge to yell in meetings, choosing between oat milk and almond milk, and trying not to strangle the printer.

So when evening comes and you ask your exhausted brain to *make one more virtuous choice*, it laughs. Silently. Then hands the mic over to your inner toddler who wants snacks and zero obligations.

This isn't a character flaw. It's neuroscience. The more decisions you make in a day, the less willpower you have left — it's called **decision fatigue**, and it's why even Barack Obama wore the same suit every day. He wanted to save willpower for the big stuff. You? You used it up deciding what kind of hummus to buy.

🍪 Exhibit A: The Cookie Paradox

In one experiment, participants were asked to resist eating cookies (cruel, right?) and then solve puzzles. The cookie-resisters gave up on the puzzles much faster than those who weren't tempted. Conclusion? *Resisting cookies = drained willpower = reduced problem-solving.* (Also: never do puzzles hungry.)

So if you're sitting there saying, "I don't know why I never stick to journaling!" — it's not that you lack discipline. You're just dealing with a brain that used all its willpower holding back from eating six Oreos earlier.

⚗ So What Works Instead of Willpower?

Systems. Routines. Traps — the good kind.

Instead of relying on daily motivation, set up your environment so journaling becomes automatic. Put your journal on your pillow. Or schedule a journaling reminder right before your favorite TV show — no journaling, no "Succession." This isn't cheating. It's *designing for success*.

Think of journaling not as a test of character, but as brushing your teeth. You don't stand in front of the sink every night thinking, "Do I feel inspired to brush tonight?" No. You just... brush. That's what a good journaling habit should feel like — *unsexy but automatic.*

💡 Real-Life Example: Kevin vs. the Morning Journal

Kevin, a graphic designer, decided to write every morning before work. Day 1: success. Day 2: meh, okay. Day 3: accidentally scrolled Twitter for 42 minutes. Day 4: breakfast won. Day 5: existential crisis over font choices.

But then Kevin moved his journal next to the coffee maker and wrote while the coffee brewed. No willpower required. Now he has 67 straight days of entries, and one of them is just "I hate my boss." Still counts

🎯 The Takeaway

Willpower is a sugar rush — short, unreliable, and gone when you need it most. The real magic is in *systems* that make journaling the path of least resistance.

So don't beat yourself up. Don't wait for the perfect moment of inspiration. Just set a trap your future self will walk right into. A journal next to your toothbrush. A pen on your pillow. A reminder called "Don't be dramatic, just write."

And remember: you're not lazy — you're just living in a world full of distractions, carbs, and autoplay.

Start So Small It's Silly

(Because even ants don't start with Everest)

Let's say you've decided to start journaling. Excellent! You picture a quiet corner, a hot cup of tea, jazz in the background, and you pouring your soul onto the page in a glorious outpouring of wisdom, wit, and poetic introspection.

And then... nothing.

You sit down, pen in hand, and your brain goes: "Let's organize our sock drawer instead."

Here's the truth: **we tend to start too big**, aiming for grandeur instead of *groove*. But habits aren't born from inspiration — they're built from repetition. And the best way to repeat something? Make it *so small, it's silly not to do it.*

🐢 The Power of the Tiny Start

Want to start journaling? Don't plan a 30-minute reflective deep dive into your soul. Plan to write **one sentence**. Or a phrase. Or even just today's date. That's not laziness — it's *strategy*.

Why? Because momentum is magic. One sentence often turns into two. One word might lead to a full paragraph. But even if it doesn't — *you've still won*. You showed up. You *kept the streak alive*. And in the world of habits, **a tiny win beats a big failure** every time.

💼 Anjali an HR Manager

Anjali, an overachieving HR professional, once decided to write a daily gratitude journal. Day 1: she wrote a full page about how much she appreciated indoor plumbing. Day 2: half a page about her dog's eyebrows. Day 3: nothing. Day 4: felt guilty. Day 5: started journaling about why she was a failure. Day 6: ice cream therapy.

Then she tried a new tactic: she committed to just **one sentence a day**. Sometimes it was as simple as "Coffee was hot. I am grateful." But she kept going — and now, six months later, she's filled an entire journal. One sentence at a time.

🧘 Start Silly, Stay Consistent

Let's say your first journal entry is:

"Today I ate a mango."

That's it. Nothing spiritual, no Shakespearean insight. But here's the catch — you *showed up*. And the next day? Maybe you'll write:

"Still thinking about that mango."

Eventually, you'll write something meaningful — or at least meme-worthy. But it starts with **permission to be ridiculous**.

📖 There's Science Here Too

In habit psychology, this is called the **"Minimum Viable Effort"**. It tricks your brain into lowering resistance. Your mind doesn't freak out over a 3-second task. You don't need motivation for silly things. You just do them.

Want to floss your teeth? Start with one tooth. Want to run a marathon? Put on your shoes. Want to start journaling? Open the notebook. Maybe draw a sad potato. Congratulations — you've begun.

🐶 Jay and the One-Word Journal

Jay, a busy dog trainer, never had time to journal. He told himself, "If I don't have 15 minutes, what's the point?" So he did nothing. Then he decided to lower the bar — *all the way down*. He'd write **one word** a day. Sometimes it was "tired." Sometimes "hairy" (that one made sense once). But he did it for 100 straight days. One day he accidentally wrote a whole page and scared himself. Progress!

🖼 The Takeaway

Forget big goals. Forget perfect conditions. Begin so small, so silly, that you laugh at how easy it is. The goal isn't to write *well* — it's to write *at all*. The rest comes later.

And hey, if all you write today is:

"Started. Still silly."

—you're doing it right.

From Silly to Systematic

So you've embraced the silly. You've written "banana" in your journal and called it a win. Bravo! But now what? Do we just keep scribbling snack names forever?

Not quite.

Once you've got a tiny habit going — even if it's one word, one sentence, or one squiggly doodle of your co-worker's haircut — the next magic move is this: **stack it onto something**, **track your wins**, and most importantly, **celebrate like you just published a bestseller**.

Because tiny habits don't grow up on their own. They need a *support system*. And in the next section, we're building exactly that. Buckle up — it's time to **Stack It, Track It, and Celebrate It**.

Stack It, Track It, Celebrate It

Because your brain is a puppy and it deserves treats.

So you've started small. You've journaled something like "My sandwich was adequate." You're on the path. But now comes the tricky part: **consistency**.

Enter the holy trinity of habit-building:

1. **Stack it**
2. **Track it**
3. **Celebrate it**

Let's break it down — with examples, obviously.

🎁 1. Stack It — aka Habit Piggybacking

Habit stacking is the art of gluing your new habit (journaling) to something you already *always* do — like brushing your teeth, boiling your morning coffee, or complaining about the group chat.

Real-life example:

Nina, a dentist, decided to journal **after she brushed her teeth** every night. Her rule? "No toothpaste, no truthpaste." She'd write one line while still in her bathroom mirror glow. That one line often turned into a mini memoir about her day, and sometimes a poem about molars. Either way, she showed up.

Habit stacking works because your brain likes patterns. If it knows "after X, I do Y," it starts to *expect* it. Like how your dog mysteriously knows it's walk time before you've said a word.

☑ 2. Track It — aka the Don't-Break-the-Chain Method

Humans are weird. We'll walk 10,000 steps just because our watch told us to. That's why **tracking your journaling streak —** even if it's just a tiny ☑ on a calendar — is pure magic.

Real-life example:

Karan, a self-confessed spreadsheet nerd, made a color-coded Excel journal tracker with formulas, emojis, and conditional formatting. It was so extra, his journal entries were sometimes just "=TODAY() is a good day." But guess what? He kept it going for 73 days straight — and then rewarded himself with a pizza. Which he also tracked.

Tracking = momentum. And momentum = confidence.

🎉 3. Celebrate It — aka Train Your Inner Labrador

When a puppy sits on command, you give it a treat. Your brain works the same way. Every time you journal, **reward yourself**.

Doesn't have to be big — a fist pump, a little happy dance, or a victory lap around your kitchen will do.

Real-life example:

Ritika, a stressed-out intern, decided to reward each journaling session with a single square of chocolate. This worked beautifully until Day 14 when she accidentally ate the whole bar and journaled, "This is fine." But hey — habit still intact.

Celebrating reinforces the behaviour. It tells your brain, "That thing I just did? That felt good. Let's do it again." And over time, your silly little habit turns into a thing you *crave* — like Wi-Fi or mildly passive-aggressive memes.

⚒ Putting It All Together

Let's say your stack is:

After coffee → write one sentence → tick calendar.

You've just built a micro-routine that's:

- Anchored in reality
- Easy to track
- Fun to repeat

It might feel tiny. But remember: you don't build a house by throwing bricks in a field. You **lay them down**, one after the other, until — ta-da! — you've got something cozy and totally Instagrammable.

3. What to Do When You Miss a Day

Because you're human, not a journaling robot.

So, you missed a day. Maybe even three. Maybe an entire week. Congratulations! You are now officially... normal.

Let's clear something up: **missing a day doesn't mean you've failed**. It just means... life happened. Maybe your kid got the flu. Maybe you binge-watched a baking show and got emotionally invested in sourdough. Or maybe, just maybe, you forgot. That's not a crime. That's a Tuesday.

Here's what NOT to do:

- Don't declare your journaling habit dead.
- Don't tear up your notebook in dramatic shame.
- Don't tweet "I am a failure. Send snacks."

Here's what TO do:

1. Wipe the Slate

Just pick up where you left off. No need to catch up on every day you missed. This isn't school. Nobody's grading you.

2. Talk to Yourself Like a Nice Person

Replace "Ugh, I messed up again" with "Cool, let's start fresh." Be the kind friend you'd want during a slump, not a moody gym coach from an '80s movie.

3. Reconnect with Your *Why*

Ask yourself: Why did I start this in the first place? To reflect? To de-stress? To stop yelling at the toaster? Revisit your reason — it's still there, waiting patiently like a golden retriever.

Real-life example:

Amit missed two weeks of journaling because... well, cricket. When he came back, he simply wrote: *"Back. Still awesome."* That's it. That's all it takes.

Chapter Summary:
Making It a Habit

This chapter shatters the myth that willpower alone can sustain a journaling habit. Turns out, you're not lazy — you're just human, and living in a world full of distractions, dessert, and documentary rabbit holes. The brain, wired for efficiency, often defaults to easier pleasures than journaling (like Googling "Are penguins monogamous?" — *monogamous* meaning: having only one mate at a time). This chapter argues for systems, not shame.

Readers are encouraged to build "good traps" — placing journals near coffee makers or next to pillows, making journaling as automatic as brushing your teeth. Through funny, relatable stories (like Kevin, who journaled while his coffee brewed, or Nina, who journaled post-toothbrush), the chapter emphasizes that small, consistent actions win over grand, inconsistent efforts.

The secret? Start so small it's silly. One sentence. One word. Even "Today I ate a mango." That's enough. Because once you show up, momentum does the rest. You also learn the holy trinity of habit building — **Stack It, Track It, Celebrate It**. Attach journaling to an existing habit, track your streak like it's a badge of honor, and celebrate each win (even if it's with a chocolate square that turns into the whole bar — we've all been there).

And if you miss a day (or ten)? Welcome to the club. The chapter offers a guilt-free reentry plan, reminding you: no backfilling, no drama. Just turn the page and begin again. With kindness.

Packed with humor, neuroscience, and bite-sized tools, Chapter 5 is a pep talk in disguise — nudging you to build a journaling habit not through discipline, but through design. Because the best journaling practice isn't perfect — it's the one you actually return to.

🔔 Mini Call to Action:

Place your journal somewhere it *can't* be ignored — next to your toothbrush, beside your coffee mug, or even on your pillow. Write just one word. One sentence. "I'm here." "Mango." "Tired but trying." Whatever it is, start small, start silly, but start today. Then do it again tomorrow. Not because you have superhuman willpower — but because you made it easy, made it yours, and made it kind. Turn the page. Begin again. You've got this.

🖼 What's Next?

So, you've done it. You've built the habit. You've scribbled "I need coffee" enough times to make it your unofficial mantra. Maybe you've even tracked a 12-day streak, rewarded yourself with a slice of cake (or three), and fist-pumped in the mirror after every journal entry.

But now you're wondering... *is this it?*

Because while consistency is great (and trust me, your future self is already sending you a high-five), it's time to go beyond the act of journaling — and dive into the **impact** of journaling.

You're not just filling pages. You're building self-awareness, spotting patterns, and discovering that your thoughts aren't just noise — they're clues.

In the next chapter, we shift gears — from **"How do I keep writing?"** to **"What can my writing reveal?"**

This is where your journal stops being a diary and starts becoming a **mirror**, a **coach**, and even a **compass**. Let's turn that habit into insight — and that scribble into something powerful.

Onward to Chapter 6: **Getting More from the Practice**.

Time to move from "I journal" to "I *grow* through journaling."

Chapter 6

Getting More from the Practice

How to turn words into wisdom (without needing incense or enlightenment).

1. Ask Better Questions

Because "What did I eat today?" is not the soul-searching you think it is.

Let's be honest — most people's journals read like the world's least interesting shopping list.

"Woke up. Brushed teeth. Had coffee. Got irritated in traffic. Ate lunch. Scrolled Instagram. Regretted nothing and everything. Slept."

There's nothing wrong with documenting your day. But if that's **all** your journaling practice consists of, you're basically just keeping a really dull alibi.

The secret to deeper journaling? Ask better questions.

Because better questions lead to better thoughts. Better thoughts lead to better choices. And better choices… well, sometimes they lead to kale, but let's not get ahead of ourselves.

.? Why "What Did I Do Today?" Isn't Enough

Let's take a common question: *"What did I do today?"*

Now, unless you're James Bond or a traveling magician, the answer is probably... not that thrilling. Even if you're busy, it's just a to-do list in past tense.

But tweak it to:

☞ **"What gave me energy today?"**

...and suddenly, we've got *insight*. You're not just tracking activities — you're tracking impact.

Try it for a week. You might discover:

- Watching squirrels for five minutes gave you more peace than two hours of forced networking.
- A phone call with your cousin actually recharged you more than three coffees.
- That passive-aggressive Zoom meeting left you emotionally bankrupt.

This question helps you identify **what actually nourishes you**, not just what filled your calendar.

⊙ Raj and the "Avoidance Audit"

Now let's talk about **Raj** — someone who considered himself "fairly self-aware" because he once read the back cover of *The Power of Now*.

Raj was feeling off. Sluggish. Cranky. Like his soul was buffering.

So instead of journaling "I'm tired again," he tried a new question:

👉 **"What am I avoiding?"**

Turns out:

- He was avoiding a hard conversation with his roommate (who kept eating his cheese).

- He was avoiding finishing his tax returns (filed under: emotional labor).

- And yes, he discovered an expired gym membership — not because he missed working out, but because the gym had started calling him like a jilted ex.

Asking "What am I avoiding?" turned his journal from a venting outlet into a **clarity mirror**. He didn't magically become a productivity ninja, but he *did* have the talk, pay his taxes, and break up with the gym properly.

🔘 Try These Instead: The Juicier Questions

Here are some *actually useful* alternatives to "What did I do today?" that can spice up your journal — and your self-awareness.

🔋 *"What drained me today?"*

Identify energy vampires (spoiler: sometimes it's a WhatsApp group).

📝 *Example: Tara realized her daily 'five-minute' scroll on real estate listings left her convinced she needed to sell everything and buy a goat farm.*

🥛 *"What did I say 'yes' to that I didn't want to?"*

Boundaries alert!

📝 *Example: Mike journaled that he said yes to organizing a team event because "no one else volunteered." Then wrote in all caps: NEVER AGAIN, STEPHANIE.*

🌱 *"What made me feel like myself today?"*

A reminder that joy often comes in small, weird doses.

📝 *Example: Leena felt most like herself when she danced in socks to 2000s pop while making dal. Her journal entry: "Nelly + cumin = my true self."*

🦉 *"What did I learn today that surprised me?"*

Turns each day into a discovery, not just survival.

📝 *Example: Arjun learned that lemon juice doesn't work on ink stains. His shirt — and ego — never fully recovered.*

💡 Why These Questions Matter

Journaling is like talking to your inner GPS. But if you only ask yes-or-no questions like "Did I get everything done?", you're not giving yourself a chance to **recalculate the route**.

Better questions move you from **reporting mode to reflective mode**.

From *"This happened"* to *"This mattered."*

They shine a light on the **underlying emotions, desires, fears, and values** that run quietly in the background of your daily life — like that one neighbour who mysteriously vacuums at 3 a.m.

⚒ Tools of the Trade: Keep It Fun, Not Formal

You don't need a fancy journal, calligraphy pens, or an "enchanted ritual corner." Just a notebook and the willingness to be real.

Try this:

- Pick one better question per day.

- Keep your answers short — even 3 lines can be gold.

- Revisit a few at the end of the week. You might laugh. You might wince. You might say, "Wow, I've eaten a lot of toast."

◎ Real Life, Real Talk

Sometimes your journal answer will be profound.

"What gave me energy today?" — *"Helping my friend without expecting anything in return."*

Sometimes it'll be chaotic.

"What am I avoiding?" — *"Confronting the fact that I think the plants in my office judge me."*

Both are valid. You're not writing for a Pulitzer — you're writing for **you**.

☑ Final Takeaway

Better questions are tiny keys.

They open doors in your brain you didn't know were closed.

And let's face it — if your journal isn't making you pause, smile, cringe, or cackle occasionally... are you even doing it right?

📣 Mini Call to Action:

Tonight, ask one new question. Not what you *did*, but what you *felt*, *noticed*, or *avoided*.

Write whatever comes out — even if it's "I avoided flossing again."

Because the goal isn't perfection — it's **awareness**. And maybe, just maybe, fewer expired gym memberships.

2. Use the Three Why Technique

Because sometimes the first answer is just your ego in a tuxedo.

You know that feeling when someone asks, "Why do you want that job?" and you reply with something noble like, "To make an impact," when the truth is… you just want a better chair and fewer Slack messages?

Yeah. That's **why we need the Three Why Technique**.

This technique is deceptively simple:

Ask "Why?" three times in a row.

Sounds like a toddler's favourite game, but it's secretly a Jedi mind trick for adults.

🧠 What Is the Three Why Technique?

It's a method to move past surface-level answers into the juicy center of your motivations. Think of it like peeling an onion, except it's your psyche — and yes, it might make you cry.

Here's how it works:

1. **Ask a question.**

    Example: "Why do I want to start journaling regularly?"

2. **Answer it honestly.**

    "Because I want to be more mindful."

3. **Ask why *again*.**

    "Why do I want to be more mindful?"

4. **Keep going.**

    "Because I feel like life is rushing past me and I'm missing it."

BOOM. There it is. Real reason. Not to impress your therapist. Not to post a photo of your latte next to a leather-bound journal. But because you want to feel like you're actually *living* your life.

👨‍💼 Case Study: Varun's Dream of Being "CEO Material"

Varun was journaling about his career ambitions. He wrote:

Q: Why do I want to be a CEO?
A: Because I want to lead a company.

Q: Why do I want to lead a company?
A: Because I want to make big decisions.

Q: Why do I want to make big decisions?
A: Because... honestly, I want my dad to stop introducing me at weddings as "still figuring it out."

🎯 Aha! *That's* the real juice.

By the third "why," Varun discovered that his CEO dream wasn't just about boardrooms and PowerPoints — it was tangled up in self-worth, family expectations, and the ghost of his cousin who started a fintech app.

Now, does this mean he shouldn't aim for CEO? Not at all. But now he knows **what's driving him** — and he can decide if that's a fuel he wants to keep using.

🧁 Neha and the Case of the Late-Night Baking

Neha, a freelance designer, started baking elaborate cakes at 11 p.m.

Her journal entry:

"Why do I bake at night?"

A: Because I find it relaxing.

"Why do I find it relaxing?"

A: Because it's my time. No emails, no clients, no one to please.

"Why do I crave that time so much?"

A: Because during the day, I don't feel like I'm in control of anything.

Boom again.

What looked like quirky behaviour (midnight cakes) was actually a desperate grab at autonomy. She wasn't just craving sugar — she was craving **sovereignty**.

Once she realized that, she started restructuring her daytime boundaries — and still baked, but now during reasonable hours. Her sourdough starter still thinks it's in a toxic relationship, but Neha's thriving.

✄ How to Use the Technique Without Overthinking Your Grocery List

Here's how you can apply this in your journaling:

1. **Pick any statement about your day, habit, or desire.**

   Example: "I want to work out more."

2. **Write your first answer.**

   Don't overthink. Go with the first thing that comes to mind.

3. **Ask why again — twice more.**

   Each time, pause, breathe, and go a bit deeper.

The magic usually happens around the **second or third answer**. Sometimes the first one is your polite, socially acceptable self. But the third one? That's the one who snacks at midnight in a hoodie and tells the truth.

☺ Humor Warning: It Gets Weird Fast

Example:

"Why did I binge five episodes of a baking show last night?"

1. Because I was tired.

2. Because my brain was fried from work.

3. Because watching people frost cupcakes makes me believe there is goodness in the world.

And that's valid! Sometimes the third "why" leads you to poetic, hilarious, or oddly moving places. Don't judge your answers — they're all little breadcrumbs leading to self-awareness.

🐄 Why It Works

The Three Why Technique works because it *disarms your default thinking*.

We're masters of rationalizing:

"I need a new phone because it's on sale."

No. You need a new phone because your current one reminds you of your ex and also autocorrects "Namaste" to "Namasteyyyy."

This method strips away the noise and gives you insight into your real motivations — the ones beneath the status updates and half-hearted resolutions.

💧 Real-Life Uses

- **Decision making:** Why do I want to say yes to this opportunity?
- **Emotional check-ins:** Why am I irritated today?
- **Goal setting:** Why do I care about this resolution?
- **Behavior patterns:** Why do I keep scrolling Instagram instead of sleeping?

You don't need to Three-Why everything. You're not an existential detective. But applying it to even one part of your life — consistently — can *radically* change the way you act and think.

✳ A Few Prompts to Get You Started

- Why am I resisting something I know is good for me?
- Why did I react the way I did in that conversation?

- Why do I want more free time?
- Why do I want to journal in the first place?

🧘 📷 Tip: Journal First, Analyze Later

Don't worry if your answers feel messy, contradictory, or silly. Journaling isn't a TED Talk. It's a sandbox. Let yourself play. Let your answers contradict each other. That's not failure — that's *being human*

Questions you can try – Library of questions

Here's a list of **powerful, thought-provoking, and sometimes funny questions** that you can use as *reference points*, journaling prompts. These are designed to spark reflection, nudge introspection, and keep the tone aligned a style — warm, humorous, and insightful.

Deep Self-Awareness Questions

- What gave me energy today?
- What drained me today — and why did I let it?
- What am I pretending not to know?
- What am I avoiding?
- What would I do if I weren't afraid of failing?
- What belief am I carrying that might not be true anymore?
- When was the last time I felt proud — and what caused it?
- What do I complain about the most... and what am I *really* saying?

🥸 *Decision-Making Questions*

- If no one ever knew I made this choice, would I still choose it?

- Am I doing this because I want to — or because I don't want to disappoint someone?

- What does "success" actually look like *for me*?

- If I say yes to this, what am I saying no to?

😵 *For Sticky Days & Slumps*

- What small thing can I do today that Future Me will thank me for?

- What would I tell a friend in my exact situation?

- Am I tired — or uninspired?

- If I miss one day, does that erase my progress? (Spoiler: Nope.)

😄 *Silly-But-Useful Questions*

- Am I really hungry, or just bored and near a fridge?

- What's one ridiculous thing I did today that deserves applause?

- If my thoughts had a theme song today, what would it be?

- Is this a real crisis or just a WiFi issue?

✦ *Vision & Values*

- What kind of person do I want to become this year?

- How would I spend my days if I stopped trying to impress people?

- What do I want more of in my life... and what's one way to get it?

- What would a life aligned with my values *actually* look like on a Tuesday afternoon?

How to Use This Library

You don't need to answer all these. Just *flip, pick, and write*. Or laugh. Or mutter "huh, interesting."

You're building a practice, not a personality test. There are no wrong answers — only revealing ones.

You could also:

- Use one question a week to guide your journaling.

- Write rapid-fire responses without overthinking.

- Circle back to a question every month and track how your answers evolve.

📣 Final Call to Action

Tonight, try the Three Why Technique on **anything that's bugging you, exciting you, or even just confusing you**.

Don't aim for epiphanies (sudden, deep realizations or "a-ha" moments). Just aim for honesty.

And if you end up discovering that your obsession with houseplants is really about your need to nurture things you *can't* accidentally ghost — well, welcome to the club.

🕵️ 📷 Spot the Patterns

Because your journal might be trying to tell you something... repeatedly.

Journaling isn't just about recording your thoughts. It's also about reviewing them — like a Netflix recap of your own life. And let's be honest: sometimes that recap reveals plot holes, recurring characters you wish would exit stage left, and a suspiciously familiar phrase that keeps popping up like a bad jingle.

Which brings us to one of the most powerful and oddly overlooked journaling habits: **rereading your old entries.** Yes, go back and read what you wrote in the past or your past entries. Not just to cringe (though that's often unavoidable) — but to **spot the patterns** that your subconscious keeps serving up like daily specials.

The "Wait a Minute..." Effect

Maybe you keep writing things like:

- "I need a break."
- "Why do I always say yes to things I don't want to do?"
- "Back pain again. Weird."
- "Tired. Again. Might be the full moon? Or caffeine. Or life."

If that last sentence has shown up twelve times in a month, **it's probably not just the chair's fault.** (Though it *might* be time to fire the chair, too.)

Your journal, over time, becomes a highlight reel of your internal loops. Think of it like a fitness tracker — but for your emotional life. And spoiler alert: you might not be "just busy." You might be *burned out, bored,* or *secretly dreaming of living in a lighthouse far from group chats.*

Real Life Example: The Reluctant Volunteer

Let's meet Neha, a kind-hearted, chai-loving HR manager with a spreadsheet addiction. Every time someone needed help with organizing a baby shower, an office outing, or a surprise cake for someone who doesn't even like cake — Neha volunteered.

One weekend, she went through her past 3 months of journal entries and found the phrase:

"I wish someone would plan something for *me*."

It had appeared **eight times.** In different moods. On different days. Even once in all caps.

Cue epiphany (that's a fancy word for "A-ha!" moment): Neha didn't just need a break. She needed **to feel appreciated** — not just operational.

After spotting this pattern, Neha did two things:

1. She politely said "no" to three upcoming office events.
2. She took herself on a solo date to a fancy café, complete with a mystery novel, zero guilt, and two croissants.
3. That entry? It read: *"I needed this. I feel human again."*

Boom. Pattern spotted. Pattern interrupted.

Journals Don't Lie (Even When We Do)

The thing about journaling is — it's brutally honest, even when *you're not.* You may tell your coworkers you're fine, tell Instagram you're thriving, and tell your pet that you're just "in a weird mood." But your journal? That's where the truth leaks out.

- If you keep saying you're "not stressed" but have 23 entries mentioning eye twitching — congrats, Sherlock, you found a clue.

- If you keep writing about that *one friend* who "means well but drains me" — it's time to look at boundaries, not just brunch menus.

- If you notice your weekend plans often include "recovering from the week," you might not need better plans — you might need a gentler week.

Spotting the patterns isn't about judging yourself. It's about noticing. You're not trying to write a thesis. You're trying to notice that every third Tuesday, you get existential and reorganize your kitchen spice rack.

Awareness is the first step to change. The second step is doing something slightly less self-destructive.

How to Spot Patterns (Without Becoming a Detective)

1. **Set aside time.** Once a month, schedule a 30-minute journal review session. Tea helps. Snacks optional but encouraged.

2. **Highlight repeated phrases.** Look for emotions, complaints, recurring characters (hi again, Passive-Aggressive Pete), and repeated dreams or desires.

3. **Ask: "What is this trying to tell me?"** For example:

   - If "I'm overwhelmed" keeps showing up, is it your workload, your expectations, or your calendar-from-hell?

   - If "I'm bored" shows up a lot... what kind of excitement are you craving?

4. **Write a summary reflection.** Just a few lines like:

   "This month, I noticed I kept writing about feeling disconnected. Time to schedule some real connection, not just comment likes."

Humour Break: The "Helpful" Journal Entry Translator

- *"Maybe I'm just tired."* = I am running on fumes and optimism.

- *"I should drink more water."* = I am spiraling but can only control hydration.

- *"It's fine, I'm fine."* = Please send help and possibly chocolate.

Real Life Example: The Entrepreneur with Too Many Tabs

Arjun, a freelancer-slash-content-creator-slash-coffee-shop-fixture, kept ending his entries with, "Need to focus more." He thought it was about productivity. Then he reviewed his journals.

Turns out, 70% of his entries also referenced *new business ideas*. He had thirteen half-started things. No wonder he couldn't focus. He was juggling flaming torches... while skateboarding.

After spotting the pattern, Arjun chose one idea to pursue for 90 days. The rest? Parked gently in a "Maybe Later" notebook.

Within a month, Arjun wrote: *"I'm still busy, but I'm no longer scattered. It feels... sane. Is this adulthood?"*

Call to Action:

Re-read, reflect, and get curious.

Don't be afraid of what you'll find in your old pages. You might discover hidden wisdom. Or at the very least, a recurring need to change your pillow.

Circle words. Track moods. Laugh at your past self. Spot what repeats — and decide what to keep, and what to let go.

Your patterns aren't problems. They're **breadcrumbs leading to clarity.**

Awesome! Here's a **journal worksheet** called **"Spot the Patterns: A Monthly Reflection Tool"** to help track recurring themes in their entries and gently decode our own lives — with a mix of structure, humour, and self-awareness.

✺ Spot the Patterns: A Monthly Reflection Tool

Use this worksheet once a month to review your past journal entries. Find what's been echoing in your head (and life), even if it sounded like background noise. All you need is 30–45 minutes, your favourite drink, and a highlighter (optional: confetti for breakthroughs).

🗒 Step 1: Look Back

Instructions: Flip through your entries from the past 30 days. Don't read *every single word* — unless you're on a train with no Wi-Fi. Instead, skim and pause when something stands out.

☑ Highlight or underline phrases, sentences, or moments that feel:

- Emotional

- Repetitive

- Dramatic (hello, "I CAN'T DO THIS ANYMORE" in caps)

- Funny

- Off-brand for you

📝 Step 2: Make a List

Write down words, feelings, or themes that came up more than once. It can be serious or silly:

Recurring Theme	How Often?	Notes
"Tired"	7 times	Always after meetings. Coincidence? Unlikely.
"Should drink more water"	5 times	Also ate 5 bags of chips. Interesting.
"I feel invisible"	3 times	During group chats or family dinners. Hmm.
"Maybe I'm in the wrong job?"	4 times	Okay, now we're getting somewhere.

🧠 Step 3: Ask Yourself

Now reflect on the list. Try answering these:

- What's the **loudest pattern** here?

- What's the **most surprising** one?

- What do I need *more of*?

- What do I need *less of*?

- What's one small experiment I could try next month based on these insights?

🔍 Step 4: Pick Your "Clue of the Month"

Circle one insight that feels juicy. This is your clue — a gentle nudge, not a mandate.

> 🖉 *My clue of the month:*

"I need more time alone that doesn't involve doing laundry."

🌐 Bonus Round: Humor Check

Complete the sentence:

- This month, I was basically __________ in disguise.

  (e.g. "an under-caffeinated monk," "a drama queen with deadlines," "a golden retriever with burnout")

🗣 Step 5: Talk Back to the Pattern

If your journal were a friend repeating the same advice over and over, what would it be trying to say?

> 🖉 *Probably something like:*

"Hey... you keep writing about needing rest but then scroll until 1am. Let's talk."

🎯 Next Steps

Now that you've spotted the pattern:

- What's one **thing to try** next month to change it (if needed)?

- What's one **thing to celebrate** that showed up repeatedly in a *good* way?

Reframe Negative Narratives

Title: From Stuck to Strong — Shifting the Inner Script

There's a tiny voice that loves to narrate our life like it's a courtroom drama — every misstep a crime, every failure a character flaw. But here's the plot twist journaling offers: you get to rewrite that script.

We often write in frustration — "I messed it up again," "Why can't I get it right?" "I'm stuck." But what if, instead of seeing those words as a dead-end, we treated them like a draft?

Journaling allows us to pause the harsh narrative and insert one that's honest, but kinder. It doesn't mean ignoring reality — it means seeing it through a lens that includes progress, not just problems.

Real-Life Reframe: The Mic Drop Moment

A friend and reader of early drafts of this book, once showed me a page from her journal. For weeks, she'd written some variation of "I failed again." Job rejections. Missed workouts. Family arguments. Her journal was a running tab of guilt.

Then one day, I flipped to a page and saw this:

"I survived again."

Same story. Different headline.

It hit me like a mic drop.

She didn't erase the struggle. She reframed it.

She stopped journaling like a judge and started journaling like a witness — one who saw the fight and the fortitude.

Reframing isn't about sugar coating. It's about recoding. Turning:

- "I'm stuck" into "I'm figuring out what doesn't work."
- "I keep failing" into "I keep trying."
- "No progress" into "Tiny progress, barely visible, but real."

Even a one-word shift changes how it lands in your mind.

Try it:

"I'm lost." → "I'm learning." "I hate this." → "This is hard, and I'm doing it anyway."

That's power.

✍ Your Turn: Rewrite the Story

You don't need to fake optimism — just find a softer, truer angle. These prompts will help.

🏵 1. What's a recent situation where I felt like I failed?

→ Now reframe it: What did I learn, survive, or uncover?

📖 2. What negative thought keeps showing up in my mind?

→ Try writing it down, then gently challenge it. Is it 100% true?

💬 3. If this moment were a chapter title in a book about my life, what would I call it?

→ Bonus: Rewrite the title so it feels more hopeful, funny, or brave.

🎧 **4. What would I say to a close friend who wrote what I just did?**

→ Now say it to yourself. Yes, it counts.

✦ **5. One sentence to take forward from today's writing:**

→ For example: *"I survived again."*

Or *"This is tough, but I'm tougher."*

Remember, your journal isn't a log of perfection. It's the space where new language for your life begins.

Set Intentions, Not Just Reflections

"Journaling isn't just about what happened — it's also about what could."

When people think of journaling, they often picture someone staring thoughtfully out a window, scribbling down what happened that day. "I woke up tired. Drank too much coffee. Got ignored in that meeting. Ate noodles. Slept. The end."

Sure, it's helpful. But if all we ever do is report the day like an emotional weather forecast — cloudy with a chance of regret — we're missing half the magic.

Because journaling isn't just a rear view mirror. It can be a steering wheel.

From Autopsy to Intention

Reflection helps us understand the past. But intention gives us influence over the future.

Instead of ending every entry with a sigh, try ending with a sentence that sounds like a gentle nudge:

"Tomorrow, I want to feel lighter."

"Tomorrow, I want to focus on kindness."

"Tomorrow, I want to stay off my phone for one whole hour without crying."

These aren't to-do lists. They're gentle signposts for your brain. Because your mind, funny as it is, wants to solve whatever question you give it.

Tell it, "Why do I suck at everything?" — and it'll make a PowerPoint presentation titled *"Evidence."*

Tell it, "What would help me feel braver tomorrow?" — and it'll start hunting for answers.

Real-Life Example: Jim Carrey

Yes, the actor who climbed out of a fake rhino's butt in *Ace Ventura* is also famous for his journaling habit. Jim Carrey once wrote himself a $10 million check "for acting services rendered" and dated it five years into the future. He kept it in his wallet. Years later, he received exactly that amount for *Dumb and Dumber.*

Now, that may sound a bit too *vision board with glitter* for some of us. But the point isn't the money. It's that journaling helped him set an emotional and mental compass.

Whether or not the universe listens — **you** do.

Personal Example: The Smallest Intentions Matter

A few months ago, I ended a journal entry with:

"Tomorrow, I want to listen more than I speak."

That's it. No big plan. No guilt trip.

The next day, I found myself in a tense meeting, and instead of interrupting, I paused. The intention flickered into my mind, and that pause changed the entire conversation.

It wasn't magic. It wasn't flawless. But it was *different.*

And that small difference was born on the page the night before.

Set the Tone, Not Just the Record

Think of journaling like setting the music for your day.

Reflection is like looking back at yesterday's playlist — "Wow, I looped the song 'Overthinking Again' twelve times."

Intention is choosing today's track. Even if the day goes off-key, you at least began with rhythm.

Try This Prompt:

End your journaling session with a sentence that starts with:

- "Tomorrow, I want to feel..."
- "I'd like to try..."
- "I want to notice..."

- "If I could change just one thing tomorrow, it would be…"

You'll be amazed how those words stay with you, whispering in the back of your mind the next day — not as a demand, but as a quiet intention.

Final Thought:

Journaling isn't just an archive of who you were. It's a co-creator of who you're becoming.

So next time you close your notebook, don't just end with a full stop.

End with a soft arrow pointing forward.

One sentence. One aim. One tomorrow.

"The best way to predict the future is to create it."

— Abraham Lincoln

Chapter Summary:
From Reflection to Revelation

Journaling isn't just about getting thoughts out — it's about understanding, reframing, and moving forward with intention. In this chapter, we explored how to make the most of your journaling practice with five powerful tools that take your writing from surface-level to soul-level.

It starts with learning to **ask better questions**. Instead of writing bland recaps like "What did I do today?", you can switch to energizing prompts like "What gave me energy today?" or "What am I avoiding?" The quality of your questions determines the quality of your insights.

Then comes the **Three Why Technique** — a deceptively simple trick to uncover your deeper truth. By asking "Why?" three times, like a curious toddler (but with more self-awareness), you peel away surface frustrations and get to the root of your emotions.

We also looked at how to **spot the patterns** hiding in your entries. If you keep writing "I'm tired" or "I need a break," your journal may be telling you what your brain won't say out loud.

Next, we reframed inner narratives. **Reframing negativity** like "I failed" into "I survived" or "I'm learning what doesn't work" gives you back your power — and perspective.

And finally, we shifted focus to the future. By **setting intentions**, not just reflecting on the past, you direct your energy forward. Try closing entries with "Tomorrow, I want to feel..." and watch how your days begin to align with your desires.

This chapter was about sharpening your tools. Because journaling isn't just a mirror — it's also a compass. And you, dear reader, are learning to steer.

✍ Your Turn: From Reflection to Action

This week, let's experiment with taking your journaling deeper — not just recording what happened, but discovering what matters.

Day 1 – Ask a Better Question

Instead of "What did I do today?", try:

☞ *"What gave me energy today?"* or

☞ *"What drained me?"*

Write just 5–7 lines. Be curious.

Day 2 – Use the 'Three Why' Technique

Pick one emotion you felt today. Then ask "Why?" three times.

Don't overthink — just follow the thread.

Example:

"I felt anxious."

Why? "Because I have a deadline."

Why? "Because I keep procrastinating."

Why? "Because I'm scared the work won't be good enough."

Day 3 – Spot the Pattern

Re-read your last 3–5 entries. Do any words or feelings show up often?

What might they be trying to tell you?

Day 4 – Reframe a Negative Narrative

Take a thought like "I'm behind" or "I failed" — and rewrite it.

What's a more compassionate truth?

Example: *"I didn't fail. I paused. And now I'm learning to continue."*

Day 5 – Set an Intention

End today's entry with:

☞ *"Tomorrow, I want to feel…"*

And let that small sentence gently steer your next day.

You don't have to be profound. You just have to be present.

No one else will read these words. But *you* will feel them.

Keep showing up — one honest page at a time.

From Insight to Inner Strength

You've now sharpened your journaling tools — asking better questions, spotting hidden patterns, even flipping failure on its head. You've moved from scribbling out stress to actually steering your state of mind.

But now comes the real power move:

How do you use this practice not just for insight, but for inner strength?

Because here's the truth: life won't always wait for your next journal entry. Stress won't announce itself politely. Anxiety doesn't RSVP. Some days, your mind will feel like 47 browser tabs are open — and they're all playing audio.

That's where this next chapter steps in.

Think of it as your mental gym circuit — short, practical journaling workouts that help you build focus, calm, gratitude, and emotional flexibility.

This is where journaling moves from "nice-to-do" to "need-to-do."

From passive reflection to **active mental fitness**.

Let's turn the page — and turn your journal into a daily workout for the mind.

Chapter 7

Journaling for Mental Fitness

Strengthen Your Mind, One Page at a Time

Emotional Decompression

Why Your Brain Needs a Daily Cooldown

Ever finished a day feeling like your brain was a crowded WhatsApp group that never muted itself? That's what happens when we don't decompress. Thoughts pile up, emotions tangle like headphone wires, and suddenly you're weeping over an overripe banana because "life is slipping away."

Enter journaling: your brain's version of taking off tight jeans at the end of a long day.

Journaling gives emotions a place to land. It doesn't fix everything, but it stops feelings from running wild in your head like unsupervised toddlers with glitter. You write, you release. No judgment, no filter.

Real-Life Example:

Actor Kristen Bell (of *Frozen* and *The Good Place*) has openly talked about her struggles with anxiety and depression. In interviews, she's mentioned how journaling is one of her go-to tools to "let the stress out of her head and onto paper." It's not always pretty. Some days it's profound. Other days it's just, "I'm tired. I ate cake. I have regrets."

Personal Anecdote:

I once journaled an entire page complaining about a neighbour's wind chimes. They weren't particularly loud — "I was just particularly irritable. But by the time I wrote, "Maybe I'm projecting," I had laughed at myself and deflated the drama. Journaling doesn't judge. It just listens.

So go ahead, brain-dump your mess. Cry on the page. Complain. Celebrate. Process.

Think of it as emotional detox — without the celery juice.

Mood Tracking That Doesn't Feel Like Homework

How to Spot Your Emotional Weather Without a Spreadsheet

Let's be honest — traditional mood tracking can feel like... well, a school project you forgot was due. Stickers. Charts. Graphs. Some apps even ask you to rate your day with emojis. ("Hmm, was I more or today?")

But journaling? It lets you **track your mood without trying to track your mood.**

Here's the trick: don't start with "How was I feeling today?" Instead, just write your day in a few lines — and then re-read later. Patterns emerge. Maybe every Tuesday you're tense.

Maybe rainy days make you philosophical. Maybe every third meeting with Steve makes you want to move to the Himalayas.

💡 Real-Life Example:

Poet and philosopher Rainer Maria Rilke used letters and journal entries to notice when his melancholy peaked and what triggered it. He didn't "track moods" per se — but by writing daily, he started understanding his cycles of energy, inspiration, and doubt.

🌀 Personal (and embarrassing) Discovery:

I once went back through two weeks of journaling and realized I'd written "so tired today" *eight times*. My first reaction? Maybe I'm iron deficient. My second reaction? Maybe I just need to stop watching conspiracy documentaries at 1 AM. Mystery solved. (Also, aliens probably aren't in charge. Probably.)

✦ Tip:

Add a "Mood Emoji of the Day" at the end of your entry — but make it weird.

Instead of 👻 try:

"Mood: Damp toast with ambition."

Strangely accurate.

Remember, the goal isn't to diagnose yourself — it's to *notice* yourself.

Your journal becomes a gentle mirror. And sometimes, it's also a weather report:

"Cloudy with a chance of laughter."

Gratitude

Tiny Thanks, Big Shifts

→ *Rewiring the brain to notice what's working — even on days that don't.*

Gratitude journaling isn't about pretending life is perfect. It's about zooming in on the *few* things that *are* okay — even when the rest of your day feels like a group project gone wrong.

You don't need a big win to be grateful. Some days, the coffee didn't spill. The Wi-Fi worked. You remembered your friend's birthday (even if Facebook reminded you). That's enough.

⊚ Personal Practice:

Every day, I make it a point to mention *three reasons* why I'm grateful. Some days, it's deep stuff:

"I'm grateful for my health, my family, and meaningful work."

Other days, it's sheer survival:

- "My shirt didn't wrinkle."
- "Everyone actually replied to my email — on time!"
- "My housemaid came today, exactly on time, without me sending a follow-up reminder and without any last-minute plot twists."

Boom. Grateful.

The magic isn't in the *content* — it's in the *consistency*. When you do it regularly, your brain rewires to look for the good *on purpose*. You start noticing moments in real time and thinking:

"Ooh, I'll write this later."

That's gratitude training — like a mental gym rep.

💡 Real-Life Example:

Psychologist and author Dr. Martin Seligman, one of the founding fathers of positive psychology, ran studies where participants wrote down just *three good things* every night. Within weeks, their levels of optimism and well-being skyrocketed — even if nothing else in their life changed.

✦ Tip:

Try this: End your journal with:

"Today I'm grateful for…"

Even if it's "iced coffee," or "the delivery guy didn't ring the bell 37 times."

Because when your day won't listen, gratitude whispers:

"Look here — something still worked."

Micro-Meditations on Paper

Mindfulness for People Who Can't Sit Still

→ *Using short journaling bursts to feel grounded, focused, and fully present*

You know how people talk about sitting still and watching their breath like it's the most natural thing in the world?

Yeah, I'm not one of those people.

If traditional meditation makes your brain itch — welcome. This is your space. Because journaling can be *your* meditation — minus the crossed legs and chanting.

◎ Enter: Micro-Meditations on Paper.

These are tiny, intentional writing bursts (just 1–3 minutes) where you pause, breathe, and capture what's happening *right now*. Not last week. Not tomorrow. Just this moment.

Try this:

- "What am I feeling in my body right now?"
- "What's the loudest thought in my mind?"
- "What's one thing I can see, hear, and smell?"

It sounds simple — but it pulls you *into* the moment like a camera lens coming into focus.

✒ Real-Life Example:

Comedian and actor Mindy Kaling has mentioned that between shoots or meetings, she jots down quick reflections — not deep monologues, just a line or two. "It helps me reset," she says. "Like a screenshot of my brain."

Same goes for athletes like Naomi Osaka, who journal quick emotional check-ins before matches to stay grounded. They're not writing essays. They're *breathing through the pen.*

😄 Someone once Confessed:

I once tried meditating for 10 minutes. Made it to minute 3 before I started planning dinner, remembering an awkward conversation from 2012, and wondering if owls have knees. Journaling? Way better. I'm actually *there*.

📝 Tip:

Keep it short. Keep it honest. Think of it as a brain exhale.

Because sometimes, mindfulness doesn't mean silence. It means writing down what your mind is actually saying — and meeting it without judgment.

Build Your Inner Coach

Because the Critic Already Has a Megaphone

→ *Crafting a kind, wise inner voice through structured journaling.*

Let's face it — we all have that inner critic. The one who says, "You could've done better," "You're not enough," or, in my case, "Did you really need that third donut?"

It's like having a loudspeaker in your head, constantly questioning every decision you make — usually at the most inconvenient times. But here's the thing: while the critic is always ready to jump in, your inner coach is *a little more shy*.

That's where journaling comes in. With practice, you can start to drown out the negativity and create a positive, wise, and compassionate voice to guide you — instead of the constant barrage of "Why are you so lazy?"

🧠 How Journaling Helps:

By consciously shifting your journaling practice to focus on self-compassion and growth, you can build your inner coach. Every time you journal, you're essentially training that inner voice to be more like a supportive mentor and less like a judgmental parent.

For instance, instead of writing, "I didn't finish my to-do list again," try, "I didn't finish my to-do list, but I learned that I need to plan better next time."

Real-Life Example:

Marie Forleo, a successful entrepreneur and author, frequently talks about how journaling has helped her shift from self-doubt to self-confidence. She believes journaling gives her the space to quiet the negative chatter and become her own best coach. In one of her podcasts, she said, "Journaling is where I turn to when I need to give myself a pep talk. It helps me figure out the action steps I need and reminds me I've got this."

💡 Tip:

Try writing as if you're coaching a friend. You wouldn't tell your friend, "You messed up again" — you'd say, "You've got this. Let's figure out a new way forward." Practice this compassionate tone in your journaling, and soon, that supportive voice will become second nature.

Your Emotional Recovery Kit

Write Now, Bounce Back Faster

→ *Journaling as a self-first-aid when life punches low — breakups, setbacks, burnout.*

Life is great... until it's not. Sometimes, life feels like a nonstop rollercoaster — but instead of screaming in excitement, you're clutching the bar, hoping you make it to the end in one piece. Whether it's a breakup, burnout, or the 15th setback of the week, we've all been hit with the "life punch."

Here's where journaling comes in — like a first-aid kit, but instead of bandages, you get a pen and some self-compassion.

🧠 How Journaling Helps You Recover Faster:

When life knocks you down, journaling provides a safe space to process emotions, heal, and recalibrate. It allows you to express anger, frustration, and sadness without judgment. And guess what? Writing about those tough feelings actually helps you *move through them* faster.

Think about it: When we bottle up emotions, they just fester. But when we release them through writing, they lose some of their power. It's like taking the wind out of a balloon. The air doesn't go away, but it's no longer threatening to explode.

Real-Life Example:

Author **Elizabeth Gilbert**, best known for her memoir *Eat, Pray, Love*, has openly shared how journaling helped her navigate her own dark periods, especially after her divorce. In interviews, she described how writing became her emotional recovery tool: "When I started writing, I stopped feeling like I was going crazy." Journaling helped her process the grief and make sense of her feelings, and eventually, it guided her toward a renewed sense of self.

Personal Humorous Example:

I once found myself in the depths of what I called "The Great Pizza Crisis" (otherwise known as a professional setback). Much like a break-up, this setback had me feeling emotionally drained, frustrated, and a bit lost. I didn't know whether to order pizza or just wallow in my own despair. So, I grabbed my journal and wrote: "Dear Pizza, please stop being so delicious. I need emotional distance." The next thing I knew, I was ordering both pizza and chocolate — because, why not? But the key point here is that the journaling gave me the emotional space I needed to process my feelings. It allowed me to step out of the emotional fog, gain some clarity, and move forward.

📌 Tip:

Journaling isn't about fixing everything all at once — it's about creating the space to feel and heal. Write for just 10 minutes, and focus on releasing whatever is stuck inside. It's like a mental detox. You don't have to figure everything out in one sitting. Just start with one feeling and let the pen guide you.

The Five-Minute Fitness Plan

Quick Journaling Workouts for Your Mind

→ *Journaling in short bursts to recharge and refresh — mental fitness doesn't require hours.*

In today's fast-paced world, who has the time for a 60-minute journaling session every day? The truth is, you don't need hours of writing to feel the benefits of journaling — just five minutes can work wonders for your mental fitness. Think of it like the gym for your brain. Instead of long, sweaty sessions that leave you tired, you can knock out a quick mental workout in no time.

The beauty of the five-minute journaling plan is that it gives you space to check in with yourself, reframe negative thoughts, and relieve stress — all without eating up your precious time.

Real-Life Example:

Author **Tim Ferriss**, the famous productivity guru, swears by quick journaling exercises for clearing his mind and boosting focus. In his *Tools of Titans* book, Ferriss writes about using "morning pages" — a journaling method where you simply write whatever comes to mind for five minutes. He uses this to help clear mental clutter and set the tone for a productive day. It's not about writing a masterpiece; it's about getting the thoughts out of your head so you can focus on what really matters.

Humorous Insight:

I tried this once during a particularly stressful day at work. My five-minute session went something like this: "I am angry. I want pizza. Also, my pen is leaking." Okay, maybe not the deepest entry. But it did help. I managed to release some built-up tension, and I was able to focus better when I tackled my next project. Five minutes didn't solve everything, but it made me feel lighter and more present. And hey, if that's not a win, I don't know what is!

Tip:

Don't worry about writing perfectly. If you're a perfectionist, this will be your *breakthrough* moment. Five minutes means you don't have time to self-edit. Just write. The focus here is not on crafting a perfectly insightful journal entry; it's about setting your intentions for the day or releasing pent-up thoughts.

Write down whatever is on your mind. Some days it may be "I need coffee." Other days, it might be "I feel stuck, but I'm getting through it." There are no wrong answers. Five minutes of writing, even if it's just random thoughts, will help you feel grounded and connected.

Bonus Insight:

I like to treat my five-minute journaling session like a mental snack. It's a short burst of mental energy that helps me refocus, reduce stress, and take a step back. You don't need a lot of time to build mental resilience — just consistent, small efforts.

Chapter Summary:
Journaling for Mental Fitness

In this chapter, we explored how journaling isn't just a way to express thoughts—it's a powerful tool for maintaining and improving mental fitness. Just as we need physical exercise to keep our bodies strong, we need mental workouts to keep our minds sharp, resilient, and grounded.

We started by understanding how journaling helps with **emotional decompression** — releasing pent-up feelings and stress in a healthy, productive way. By giving our emotions a space to be acknowledged and processed, journaling works like a mental steam valve, easing tension and providing clarity.

Next, we explored **gratitude reps**, small exercises that train the brain to notice the positive. Even on the worst days, journaling forces us to pause and find things we can be thankful for — big or small. It's these little shifts in perspective that can make a massive difference over time.

We also touched on how **micro-meditations** through journaling offer quick bursts of mindfulness. These short writing sessions allow us to stay present, recalibrate, and refocus during chaotic days. Similarly, **building your inner coach** through structured journaling helps us replace the loud inner critic with a wise, compassionate voice. This fosters self-acceptance and mental strength.

Finally, we discussed **your emotional recovery kit**, where journaling serves as an essential first-aid tool when life throws setbacks our way. Whether it's a breakup, burnout, or unexpected stress, journaling helps you process, heal, and bounce back faster.

Call to Action

Now it's time to put these journaling strategies into practice. For the next week, dedicate just 5 minutes each day to journaling with a mental fitness goal in mind. Ask yourself, "What will make my mind stronger today/tomorrow?" Start small and watch how your journal becomes not just a record, but a tool for transformation.

From Strength to Strategy

As we've seen, journaling can significantly boost mental fitness, providing clarity, grounding, and emotional resilience. However, like any powerful tool, journaling comes with its own set of challenges. It's not always easy to find the time, the energy, or even the motivation to keep writing consistently.

But that's okay — because in the next chapter, we're diving into the common challenges many face with journaling and how to overcome them. Whether it's battling procrastination, overcoming the blank page, or dealing with those inevitable days when journaling feels like a chore, we'll explore smart fixes to help you stay on track.

After all, mental fitness is about consistency, not perfection. And with the right strategies, you can turn your journaling practice into something sustainable and meaningful.

Chapter 8

Common Challenges and Smart Fixes

1. "I Don't Have Time"

Reality Check: You do. But journaling needs to fit *your* life, not some ideal routine.

Fix: Micro-journaling. Three lines. Two minutes. One emotion.

Let's get honest: saying "I don't have time" is often code for "This feels optional right now." And that's okay. We all have that drawer of well-intentioned habits we never got around to — learning Spanish, or figuring out what "quinoa" really is.

Journaling can often feel like something we'll do "someday."

Someday... when the house is quiet.

Someday... when the to-do list is done.

Someday... when I magically become the type of person who does yoga at sunrise.

But here's the twist: *that day never arrives.*

Life doesn't slow down and hand you journaling time like a VIP pass. You have to sneak it in the way you sneak snacks into movie theatres — quietly, strategically, and with great commitment.

Real-Life Example:

I once asked a friend — a parent of two toddlers and a full-time working professional — when she journals. Her response?

"Between Netflix episodes. I get eight-minute windows. That's when I write down what part of my soul just got trampled and what part found unexpected joy."

That's journaling. Not in a fancy chair with jazz music, but crouched beside a plastic toy kitchen set, scribbling feelings next to spilled apple juice.

The Myth of the Perfect Window

If you're waiting for an hour of silence and a freshly brewed herbal tea, you'll wait forever. Journaling doesn't need *more* time — it needs *anchored time.*

Anchored time = tying it to something you *already* do.

- Just brushed your teeth? Write one line.
- Waiting for your coffee to brew? Write one line.
- Sat down before your first Zoom call? Write one line.

We're not talking about a whole page here. Start with this:

"Today I feel _______ because _______."

OR

"Right now, I need _______ more than anything."

That's it.

The 2-Minute Trick

Studies show that even writing for two minutes a day can reduce anxiety and improve mood. Not because you solved your life — but because you showed up for yourself.

Here's a mini journaling prompt you can finish *while waiting for an Instagram reel to load*:

"One thing that surprised me today was ________."

You don't need a ritual. You don't need a routine. You just need a pause.

Micro-Journaling Magic

Try this 3-line formula:

1. One thing that made me smile
2. One thing that annoyed me
3. One thing I'm hoping for tomorrow

It takes 90 seconds. Less than the time it takes to microwave popcorn or lose your willpower on Swiggy.

The Humorous Reality

I once set aside 30 minutes to journal. Lit a candle. Made herbal tea. Put on ambient rain sounds.

Then I spent 29 minutes setting up the vibe and 1 minute writing:

"Too many candles. This feels like I'm summoning spirits. Abort."

Lesson learned: fancy setups don't guarantee deep journaling. *Small consistent setups do.*

Final Tip:

If you truly feel like there's "no time," try **voice journaling** on your commute or while folding laundry. Just open your phone recorder and talk for 2 minutes. You'll be amazed what comes out when you aren't overthinking it.

Reframe It:

Instead of saying "I don't have time to journal," try:

"I can give myself two minutes to check in with myself today."

That's not indulgent. That's necessary.

Because if you don't make time to reflect — life will just keep running, and you'll keep chasing.

Start small. Start scrappy. Start *anyway*.

You'll be surprised how much space two minutes can create.

"I Don't Know What to Write"

Reality Check: It's not about knowing *what* to write. It's about being willing to start.

Fix: Use simple prompts, repeat yourself, and lower the bar till you trip over it.

Ah yes, the great journaling paralysis: staring at a blank page as if it's auditioning to be your therapist, life coach, and spiritual guru — all in one. You sit there with a fancy pen and a hopeful heart... and your brain decides to play dead.

"Nothing to say," it shrugs.

Meanwhile, you've had 27 conversations in your head since breakfast, including one about whether your neighbour's dog is judging your recycling habits.

You have *plenty* to say. You just don't know how to begin.

Real-Life Example:

One client of mine once wrote the words:

"This is dumb. I have nothing to say. Why am I doing this?"

Then she paused. Then she kept going:

"Okay, maybe I'm mad about the thing my boss said in that meeting. But also, why did it sting so much? Maybe I'm tired. Or just feel unseen. I don't know. But I needed to write this."

Boom. A whole page — and some solid insight — from *"this is dumb."*

Sometimes, "I don't know what to write" is actually the *first sentence you should write.*

The "Bad Entry" Rule

Let yourself write a bad journal entry. Let it be boring. Let it be whiny. Let it be full of random, snack-related thoughts.

Here's mine from a Tuesday afternoon:

"I don't want to write, but I also don't want to scroll mindlessly. So this is me choosing the lesser evil. Today I had excellent chole bhature. I feel guilty about nothing and everything. Also, my feet are cold. Okay, now I feel better."

That's not profound. It's not wise. But it was *real.* And it cleared space in my head.

Repeat Yourself. It's Fine.

You don't need a new insight every day. You don't need to be *interesting* to be *honest.*

If you've written "I'm overwhelmed" ten times this week, guess what? Your brain is sending a message. Your journal is just holding the megaphone.

You're not failing. You're noticing.

Prompts That Never Fail

If you're truly stuck, try these:

- "Right now, I feel…"
- "Today, I noticed…"
- "One thing that annoyed me today…"
- "If I could press pause on something, it would be…"
- "I wish someone would just tell me…"

Even if all you write is three fragmented thoughts and a complaint about your internet speed — *that counts.*

Humorous Insight:

I once tried a journaling app that suggested, "Write about the scent of your childhood." I stared at the screen and wrote:

"Smelled like Vicks "

Sometimes, even odd prompts get you somewhere. (Also, shoutout to Vicks for carrying us through fevers *and* feelings.)

The Shower Principle

You know how you get brilliant ideas in the shower, but they vanish once you towel off?

Journaling catches those thoughts *before* they evaporate. It's not about catching the *right* thoughts — it's about catching *any* thoughts before the day swallows them.

Final Tip:

Set a timer for 5 minutes. Write the worst, most rambling nonsense you can. Vent. Ramble. Whine. Praise biryani. End mid-sentence.

Do this for 5 days. You'll stop fearing the blank page. Because it won't be blank anymore — it'll be yours.

Reframe It:

Instead of thinking, "I don't know what to write," try:

"Let me write the first sentence badly and see what happens."

That's the trick. You don't need the *right* words.

You just need the *first* ones.

Once you start — the page will meet you halfway.

"My Journal Is Too Messy/Too Negative/Too Whiny"

Truth Bomb: Your journal is not a brochure. It's a brain dump. It's supposed to be messy, whiny, honest, and gloriously unfiltered.

Let's get this out of the way: your journal is not being judged by a literary agent. You are not auditioning for Oprah's SuperSoul Sunday (unless you are — in which case, good luck). Your journal is your *mental compost bin* — it's where you throw the scraps so something beautiful can eventually grow.

And yet, many people close the cover of their journal, look at what they just wrote, and wince.

"Why am I always complaining?"

"This sounds so negative."

"Ugh, my handwriting looks like it's been chewed by a goat."

Newsflash: That's *exactly* what journals are for. If it came out neat, polished, and filled with Pinterest-worthy affirmations, it wouldn't be a journal. It would be a corporate annual report.

Real-Life Example:

A friend once told me she stopped journaling because she felt "toxic energy" reading her own entries. She was writing only when she was upset — so naturally, it read like an angry soap opera written by a tired therapist.

Then one day, she wrote:

"Maybe I'm not negative — maybe this is where I *park* my negativity so I don't carry it around all day."

Boom. That one line changed her entire relationship with journaling. She began to see her journal as a detox chamber, not a personality test.

Let's Normalize the Whining

Imagine this: you've had a long day. You sit with a friend and start venting. You say, "Ugh, today was awful. I spilled coffee on my laptop, my boss micromanaged me, and I think I sprained my dignity in a team meeting."

Now imagine your friend says, "Wow. You sound really negative. Please try to be more grateful."

You'd never talk to them again.

But you say that to *yourself* after journaling? Nope. Not today. Journaling isn't where you *filter* your truth. It's where you *face* it.

But What About "Manifestation"?

There's a trend going around that says you should only write *positive* things in your journal — to attract good vibes.

Look, if that works for you, great. But forcing positivity is just emotional Botox. You're smoothing over what needs to be expressed. Your brain knows the truth — and it's dying for a space to let it out.

Let the truth show up messy and un showered. Later, you can tidy it up. But first, let it be.

Humorous Insight:

I once flipped through an old journal and thought, "Wow, who is this dramatic, overthinking person?" Then I realized — it was me. Writing about how a lizard in my room was a metaphor for how life was closing in on me.

Am I proud? Not exactly. How did I feel reading that old journal entry?

Mixed feelings. Amused, embarrassed, surprised... and a little humbled.

Not because the metaphor was brilliant (it wasn't), but because it reminded me how real that stress felt in the moment.

Reading it now, I could see how far I'd come — even if it was just a few inches of emotional distance.

That's the gift of journaling. It doesn't just capture who you are in a moment... it quietly shows you how you've grown.

And sometimes, growth looks like realizing:

"Okay, maybe the lizard wasn't life closing in.

Maybe I just needed sleep."

Mess is Progress

You don't judge a construction site for looking chaotic. So why judge your journal?

You're under construction, too.

Tips for When It Feels "Too Negative"

- Try "vent, then validate": First, let it all out. Then end with one line of self-kindness. ("Today sucked. But I made it through.")

- Revisit with curiosity, not criticism. When you read old entries, pretend you're reading a friend's journal. Be kind.

- Allow duality. Write: "This is hard. And I'm trying." Both can be true.

Reframe It

Instead of saying,

"My journal is too whiny,"

say:

"My journal is where I'm allowed to whine so I can speak kindly the rest of the day."

Permission Slip

You are hereby granted lifelong permission to:

- Spell badly

- Vent wildly

- Be grammatically reckless

- Be honest without explanation

Your journal doesn't want your best self.

It wants your real self.

So scribble. Grumble. Cross things out. Let the page be a mirror, not a performance.

Because that's where growth begins — in the mess, not the perfection.

Privacy Panic

"What if someone reads my journal?"

→ The fear is real — but the solutions are simple (and slightly sneaky).

If there's one thing that can send a shiver down a budding journaler's spine, it's this: the thought of someone else reading their journal.

Not a bear attack. Not writer's block. Not even forgetting to close all 78 Chrome tabs.

It's that terrifying idea that your private, raw, unfiltered thoughts — about your job, your ex, your boss, your digestive system — might end up being someone else's morning read.

This fear has a name. It's called **Privacy Panic**. And it's more common than you think.

🙈 *Real-Life Worry:*

One reader told me, "I wanted to start journaling about my work stress — but my partner once read my diary in college and now I just... can't."

Another said, "My kid once doodled on my journal while I was in the bathroom. Now I hide it like it's a state secret."

Even *Anne Frank* kept her diary hidden behind a bookcase. And she had very good reasons.

But for most of us, we're not trying to hide from the Gestapo — we just want to write "I'm tired and I hate Karen from accounting" without someone highlighting it in yellow.

So what do we do?

💬 Reframe #1: You're Not Writing a Bestseller

If someone stumbles on your journal and finds a page that says "Why am I still craving paneer at 2AM?", that's not blackmail material. That's just... being human.

Not every journal entry is a scandal waiting to happen. Most of it is painfully ordinary. But ordinary thoughts deserve privacy too — because they're *yours*.

🛠️ Strategy #1: Go Code Red

Literally. Use **code words**.

Call your boss "Captain Crunch." Label your work stress as "Project X." Use abbreviations that only make sense to you. It's not about hiding everything — just scrambling it enough that no one else can decode the emotional bomb inside.

A friend of mine used to refer to their in-laws as "The Parrots." When asked why, they said, "Because they repeat themselves and eat all the fruit." Exaggerated? May be, but safe.

🛠️ Strategy #2: Go Digital & Lock It

Apps like **Day One**, **Journey**, and even a basic Google Doc with 2FA (two-factor authentication) offer solid privacy.

You can even write in a password-protected Word doc named something incredibly boring like **"Bank Statements 2012."** No one's opening that. Not even you.

Bonus: Some apps let you tag your mood with emojis. So if all you can manage is 😵 💼 🍕 , you're still emotionally expressive. Progress!

🛠️ Strategy #3: Write and Rip

Feeling truly anxious about someone reading a specific entry? Write it down *just to release it* — then destroy it.

Yes, you're allowed to **write without keeping**. Scribble it. Tear it. Burn it (responsibly). Flush it (if your plumbing agrees).

What matters is the **expression**, not the preservation.

This works especially well for temporary vents:

- "I hate everything today."
- "I am a broccoli pretending to be a human."
- "My neighbor's wind chime is ruining my inner peace."
- Let it out. Let it go.

💬 Reframe #2: Most People Are Too Busy to Read Your Deepest Fears

No offense — but your spouse, sibling, or roommate is probably too busy doom-scrolling or reheating leftovers to pore over your inner ramblings.

And if they do? That's a different conversation. Because reading someone's journal without permission isn't "curiosity" — it's a boundary issue.

🎯 Bottom Line:

Yes, privacy panic is valid. Your journal is your sanctuary. But don't let the fear of snoops stop you from reaping the incredible benefits of self-expression.

There are ways to make your practice feel safe:

- Hide it (old-school).
- Lock it (digital).
- Mask it (code words).
- Or destroy it (like a secret agent).

Journaling is about **freedom**, not fear.

And remember: If someone *does* read your entry that says "I cried in the pantry again," maybe they'll finally understand how much you needed that break.

Let your pen be honest. And let your hiding place be creative.

The Plateau Problem

"I used to love journaling. Now... it just feels meh."

It happens quietly. One day you're pouring your heart out in pages — writing about dreams, fears, that barista who smiled at you. The next? You open your journal, stare at the page, and think:

"What's the point? I've written it all before. Nothing new is happening."

Welcome to the **plateau phase** of journaling — where the initial spark fades and your once-beloved ritual feels flat, repetitive, or even pointless.

First: you're not alone. Second: it's totally normal.

Even the most committed journalers hit a phase where the practice begins to feel… stale. Not broken. Not wrong. Just not exciting anymore.

🧠 Why It Happens

1. The novelty wears off.

At the beginning, journaling feels like a revelation. Every thought you write is a new insight. You're uncovering patterns, tracking emotions, discovering what lights you up. You feel like a mix between Socrates and Brené Brown.

But after a few weeks or months, your entries start looking suspiciously similar.

"I'm tired."

"I need a break."

"Still hate my commute."

"Ate too much again."

It's easy to think: *What's the point of writing this… again?*

2. You hit the edge of awareness.

Sometimes, a plateau means you've reached a layer of understanding — and now you need new tools, new questions, or a new reason to keep going.

Think of it like the gym. If you keep lifting the same 5kg weights every day, your muscles will eventually stop growing. Journaling works the same way.

📝 Real-Life Example: Elizabeth Gilbert

Author Elizabeth Gilbert (of *Eat, Pray, Love*) is a longtime journaler. In several interviews, she's talked about how her morning pages — written every single day — sometimes feel magical, and sometimes feel like "sweeping out the mental basement."

She doesn't always have profound insights. But she keeps showing up. Why?

Because even the mundane has value. Even a plateau is part of the practice.

💡 What To Do When Journaling Feels Flat

1. Change your prompts.

Instead of asking "How was my day?", try:

- "What surprised me today?"
- "What's one thing I didn't say out loud?"
- "What am I pretending not to know?"

A fresh question can unlock a fresh path.

2. Shift your format.

- Write a letter (to your future self, your past self, your dog).
- Make a list (Top 5 wins, Top 3 regrets, 10 weird thoughts).
- Try dialogue (have a conversation with your anxiety, or your inner critic).

Shake up the structure and see what flows out.

3. Zoom out.

Revisit older entries. Look at what you wrote two months ago, or last year. You might be shocked to see how much has changed — or how much hasn't (which is also telling).

4. Accept the plateau.

Sometimes, the best way to move through a plateau... is to go *through* it.

You don't need every entry to be earth-shattering. Think of journaling like brushing your mental teeth — you're not expecting fireworks, just hygiene.

🎯 The Reframe:

A plateau doesn't mean you're failing.

It means you're moving from inspiration to *integration*.

You've gone from "Wow, journaling is amazing!" to "Okay, this is part of me now." And that's powerful.

😆 Humorous Note:

A recent plateau entry of mine just read:

"Still overthinking. Still tired. Still avoiding laundry. The universe hasn't responded to my last three journal entries. Rude."

And yet, just writing that gave me a tiny laugh. A micro-dose of truth. A flicker of light.

📌 **Remember:**

- Plateaus are part of the path.
- Progress isn't always dramatic.
- Even boring pages are brave pages.

Show up. Write the "meh." Let it be what it is.

Because sometimes, the only way forward is through the flat part — pen in hand, page by page.

"The real voyage of discovery consists not in seeking new landscapes, but in having new eyes."

— *Marcel Proust*

I Missed a Day... or a Month

Reality Check: Welcome to the club.

If there were a loyalty program for people who've "fallen off the journaling wagon," most of us would have platinum status by now. Missing a day? That's cute. Some of us have ghosted our journals for so long, we forgot which notebook we were using.

Let's get something straight: **missing a day, a week, or even a year doesn't mean you've failed.** It just means... you're human.

We begin journaling with the best intentions. Fresh notebook. Fancy pen. Candle. Spotify playlist titled "Deep Inner Work." And then, life happens.

You oversleep. You have a fight with your partner. You get sick. You binge-watch a show that you *didn't even like*. You open your journal, see the last entry dated 37 days ago, and instantly feel like you've let your entire inner self down. The guilt creeps in. The shame whispers, "You're clearly not disciplined enough." And so, we don't return — not because we don't want to, but because we feel we've broken some unspoken sacred contract with our journaling self.

Let's kill the myth: You don't owe your journal anything.

It's not your boss. It's not your disappointed grandmother. It's a tool. And tools don't judge.

Real-Life Reminder:

Actor and writer Mindy Kaling has often used humor to describe her journaling habits. In her writings and interviews, she's joked that her entries tend to wander between personal feelings, thoughts about food, and occasional apologies for not journaling more often. She's also described moments where she would restart her journaling after a gap with a simple, casual line — treating it like a conversation with an old friend rather than a formal record. Her approach reminds us that the value lies not in being perfect, but in simply showing up on the page again.

Fix: Guilt-Free Re-entry

Here's how to gently reboot your journaling habit:

1. Don't Backfill.

You missed days — don't try to go back and recreate them like a courtroom stenographer. This isn't your taxes. It's your soul. Don't try to catch up with entries titled "What I did March 4–18." You'll burn out before you begin.

Instead, flip to a fresh page. Write today's date. Start there.

Even:

"It's been a while. Here's what's on my mind today…"

That's all it takes.

2. No Apologies Required.

Your journal doesn't hold grudges. Don't write paragraphs of self-flagellation like:

"I can't believe I stopped. I was doing so well. I've failed again."

Cut the drama. Start with:

"Let's pick up where we left off."

or

"Back on the page. That's what matters."

Your journal is a **mirror**, not a judge.

3. Shrink the Barrier.

The longer you wait, the heavier the pen feels. So make it ridiculously easy. Use a post-it note. Type three lines in your phone. Write one sentence. One word, even. You're not trying to win a Pulitzer. You're re-opening a door.

4. Celebrate the Comeback.

Returning to the page isn't weakness — it's strength. Anyone can write when they feel motivated. But **returning after you've stopped?** That takes real grit.

You showed up. Again. That's resilience.

5. Make It Light.

Don't put pressure to be profound. Journaling can be funny, messy, or even mundane. Try something like:

"Today I learned that my WiFi password is harder to crack than my emotional walls. Progress?"

Bottom Line:

Missing days is part of the process. Not a bug — a feature. Your journal doesn't care how often you come. It cares that you come back.

Journaling is not about streaks. It's about **returns**.

And every time you return, you remind yourself:

"I may fall off. But I always come back."

Boredom and Burnout

When Journaling Feels Like a Chore, Not a Choice

Let's be honest — even your favourite food would start to taste bland if you had it every single day, in the same way, on the same plate. The same goes for journaling. What begins as a sacred ritual can, over time, feel like homework from a teacher who really loves feelings.

You sit down. Open your notebook. And suddenly think: "Ugh, not again."

You're not broken. You're just... bored.

Reality Check: Boredom is not failure. It's feedback.

It's your brain's way of saying, *"Hey, I need something a little spicier than 'Dear Diary, I'm overwhelmed again.'"*

Journaling, like any habit, needs variety to stay alive. If your entries are starting to feel stale — like reheated leftovers of the same old thoughts — it's time to stir things up.

My Personal Fail Moment: The Film Script That Wasn't

Once, I was so fed up with journaling the same reflections that I thought, "You know what? Let's write a movie script. Let's make this dramatic." I declared that my journal would now be a screenplay. Except I had no plot. Or characters. Or talent for screenwriting.

I wrote for 10 minutes about a mysterious hero named... Raj. His main problem? He had to complete a training module and attend three back-to-back Zoom calls. Riveting stuff.

Half a page in, I gave up. The dialogue was terrible, the pacing worse. So I closed the journal. But you know what? I counted it as a journaling win.

Because I showed up. I wrote something. Even if it was bad, off-topic, and wildly unmarketable.

And that's what matters.

"Even when it's weird, it still counts."

When It's Boring, Add Play

Here's the fix: make journaling fun again. Lower the stakes. Try themed entries:

- 🧂 *Rant Wednesdays:* Let it all out. No filters. Complain about slow walkers, Excel, or soggy toast.

- 💝 *Gratitude Fridays:* Write three oddly specific things you're thankful for — like "My housemaid came on time," or "Everyone replied to my email. Even Rajiv."

- 🐶 *Pet Perspective Days:* Write as your cat, dog, or imaginary hamster. What's *their* take on your day?

- 🎥 *Soundtrack Sunday:* Journal what your life would look like as a movie today. What's the title? The background score?

This isn't about writing better. It's about writing *differently*.

Real-Life Example: Neil Gaiman's Boredom Breaker

Author Neil Gaiman once said he gives himself only two choices when stuck: write or stare out the window. Eventually, boredom drives him back to the page. Sometimes the best way to outsmart burnout is to get *so bored* that journaling actually feels fun again.

Try giving yourself permission to do *nothing*... except journal or stare. No phone. No snacks. Just you and your pen. You'll be shocked at how quickly inspiration shows up when distraction is gone.

Also: Don't Be Afraid of Silly

Your journal doesn't need to be a literary masterpiece. It can be doodles, lists, poems, nonsense. You're not submitting it for a Pulitzer. You're using it to stay human.

So go ahead — write a haiku about your coffee. Invent a conversation between your tired brain and your overly ambitious to-do list. Journal like no one's reading... because no one is.

Final Tip: When journaling starts feeling like flossing — something you *should* do but don't enjoy — pause and play. Let weirdness in. Let go of "should." Let your journal be the one place where you can be absurd, sarcastic, poetic, petty, or profound — all in the same paragraph.

Because the only bad journaling is no journaling at all.

When You Overthink Every Sentence
(The Inner Editor vs. The Inner You)

There's a moment in every journaling journey when you sit down to write, pen hovering above the page... and freeze.

Not because you don't have anything to say — but because you're trying to say it perfectly.

You write a sentence. Cross it out. Write another. Then wonder: *Does this sound too dramatic? Too basic? Too negative? Too much?*

And just like that, journaling — which was supposed to feel like freedom — starts feeling like a high-stakes essay submission.

Reality Check: You are not writing for The Pulitzer. You're writing for peace.

The root of overthinking in journaling often comes from years of being told to write *right*. We've been taught to edit as we go. To polish. To be neat. To be quotable.

But your journal is not a publication. It's not for an audience. It's for you. And Future You really doesn't care about grammar — they care that you showed up.

The Inner Critic Has Opinions. Politely Ignore Them.

That voice in your head saying "This sounds stupid" or "You shouldn't feel that way"? That's your inner critic. And guess what — it already has a megaphone everywhere else in life.

Let your journal be the one space where it doesn't get to interrupt.

Real-Life Story:

A friend of mine once shared that it took her 25 minutes to write a three-line journal entry. Why? Because she didn't want to "sound whiny."

Finally, she gave up and wrote:

"I feel sad. That's it. No filter. Just sad."

And then she added:

"Why is that so hard to say?"

That was the real breakthrough. Not the words. But the *honesty* behind them.

Your Journal Is a Draft, Not a Declaration

Imagine if we judged our workouts by how photogenic we looked mid-burpee (a *burpee* is a full-body exercise that involves jumping, squatting, and pushing up — often leaving you panting, sweaty, and very un-Instagrammable). Ridiculous, right?

Journaling is an *emotional workout*. Sweaty, awkward, cathartic — but useful.

You're not trying to impress anyone. You're trying to meet yourself.

The Overthinker's Hacks

Here are a few practical tricks to get around the inner editor:

- **The Timer Method:** Set a timer for 5 minutes. Write non-stop until it rings. Don't lift the pen. Don't reread. Don't correct. Just go. If all you write is "This feels weird" for 5 minutes, that still counts.

- **The Ugly Entry Challenge:** Make your journal entry intentionally *bad*. Messy. Grammar errors. Slang. Text in ALL CAPS. Give yourself permission to be gloriously incoherent.

- **Write Like No One's Watching (Because No One Is):**
- Your journal is not your boss. It won't fire you. It won't post your thoughts on Instagram. It won't judge your comma placement. It's your safest space — act like it.

- **Use Code Words If You Must:** If you're scared someone might read your journal, invent nicknames or symbols. "X called again" could be enough for you to remember what it meant — and it keeps your hand moving.

Personal Example: The Journal Entry That Got Weird (and Wonderful)

I once over-edited my entry so much that I spent 20 minutes trying to describe "mild frustration."

It made no sense. But I laughed.

Final Thought: Clarity Follows the Mess

You don't write because you're clear.

You write *to* get clear.

Overthinking tries to reverse that — waiting for clarity before you start. But that's like waiting to be fit before you go to the gym.

Start messy. Stay messy. Let the clarity catch up.

"Write what should not be forgotten."

— Isabel Allende

Even if it starts clumsy. Even if it's imperfect.

Because showing up imperfectly is still showing up.

And that's what matters most.

Chapter Summary:
Common Challenges and Smart Fixes

Journaling, like any good habit, comes with its challenges. No matter how much you enjoy it at first, there will be moments when it feels like an uphill battle. The common hurdles — from lack of time to perfectionism and boredom — can all derail even the most dedicated journaler. However, understanding these challenges and learning how to overcome them is key to sustaining the habit and making journaling a lasting part of your life.

The first and most universal challenge is **lack of time**. It's easy to tell yourself that you're too busy for journaling, especially when your to-do list seems endless. But as we've learned, journaling doesn't need to take hours; it can be done in as little as five minutes. The key is making time by finding a routine that works for you, like journaling during a lunch break, while waiting for your coffee to brew, or even in the car before running into a meeting. This chapter offers several time hacks that fit journaling into your daily schedule.

Another common issue is **perfectionism**. Many people stop journaling because they feel their writing isn't good enough, or they're worried about keeping it perfect. The truth is, journaling is meant to be a personal practice, not a public performance. There's no right or wrong way to write your thoughts — and your journal doesn't need to read like a novel. It's your space to be raw and honest. If you write poorly, great! It's an opportunity to express yourself authentically. In this chapter, we explored ways to push past perfectionism and embrace imperfection in journaling.

Then there's the issue of **boredom** and **burnout**. Over time, journaling can feel like a chore, especially if you find yourself repeating the same thoughts or feeling uninspired. To keep things fresh, it's important to change things up. Try different prompts, experiment with new writing styles, or create themed days like "Rant Wednesdays" or "Gratitude Fridays." Injecting some fun and creativity back into your practice will help you avoid burnout and stay engaged.

Lastly, **privacy concerns** often hold people back from journaling. Many worry about someone reading their personal thoughts. But, as we discussed in this chapter, the key to overcoming this fear is setting boundaries. Write in a safe place, lock your journal if needed, or use a digital platform with strong privacy settings. Ultimately, journaling is for you, and nobody else has to read it unless you want them to.

Your Turn: Flip the Script on Your Roadblocks

You've met the obstacles — now it's time to outsmart them. This week, pick **just one journaling challenge** that shows up most often for you. Is it "I don't have time"? Is it "My entries sound silly"? Maybe it's "What if someone reads this?"

Whatever it is, don't ignore it — **name it**. Then write about it.

🖋 **Prompt:**

"What's the biggest reason I avoid journaling — and what's one small way I can outsmart it?"

Don't aim for perfection. Aim for one honest page. Or half. Or even one messy line.

And remember:

- Five imperfect entries beat zero perfect ones.
- A "boring" entry is still a record of your day.
- And if you missed journaling this week? Congratulations — you're human. Welcome back.

Make this the week you journal **because of** the challenge, not in spite of it.

You've got your smart fixes. Now, turn the page — and keep going.

In the previous chapter, *Common Challenges and Smart Fixes*, we addressed some common roadblocks like lack of time, perfectionism, and boredom. As we move forward, the goal is to make journaling an easy and enjoyable habit. This chapter will help you by offering templates, creative prompts, and writing exercises that make your journaling routine something to look forward to, not just another item on your to-do list. By using the tools provided in this chapter, you'll have everything you need to overcome boredom and keep your journaling practice alive.

Chapter 9

Templates, Prompts, and Ideas

Let's face it — journaling can feel repetitive if you're staring at the same blank page every day, asking yourself, "So… how do I feel today?" (Spoiler: tired. Again.) This chapter is your journaling buffet: a grab-and-go toolkit of prompts, templates, and creative techniques that help keep your practice fresh, focused, and as entertaining as it is insightful.

Because while journaling is deeply personal, having a few go-to formats makes it easier to stay consistent — especially when motivation is low or you're just plain bored. Think of this chapter as your "gym bag" filled with tools to carry into any journaling session — whether you're doing a full workout or just a five-minute stretch.

A Collection of Daily Prompts: Simple Sparks with Surprising Power

These prompts are your warm-up drills — quick, focused, and capable of pulling surprising insights from a single sentence. They're great for when you have only five minutes, but still want to anchor your mind.

They not only help bypass the blank-page panic, they make you stick with this good habit. You don't need a perfect story or profound insight — just a nudge. One sentence. One thought. One spark.

Examples:

- What made me feel alive today?
- What's one thing I learned about myself this week?
- What am I tolerating that I shouldn't be?
- What would I do if I wasn't afraid?
- What's something I wish someone would say to me right now?

These prompts sound simple — but don't underestimate them. They often unlock the real stuff. The kind of clarity that doesn't always come when you try too hard.

Why This Works: Because prompts remove pressure. You don't have to think of a "topic." You don't need to be poetic or insightful. You just answer the question in front of you.

Pro Tip: Print out 31 prompts, fold them into a jar, and draw one out each day. Bonus dopamine included. It turns reflection into a lucky dip.

Feeling Fancy? Color code your prompts — yellow for energizers, blue for emotional check-ins, red for creative ones. You now have a whole journaling palette.

Humorous Hack: One reader told me she turned these prompts into a party game. Each friend picked a prompt from the jar and had to write one sentence. Her favourite entry? "What would I do if I weren't afraid?" — the answer: "Finally tell my roommate that it was me who dropped her mobile."

That's the beauty of prompts. They get you writing. And when you're writing, you're listening to yourself.

So next time you're stuck, don't try to write everything. Just answer something.

31 Daily Prompts Jar

1. What made me feel most alive today?
2. What am I avoiding — and why?
3. What do I wish someone would say to me right now?
4. If today had a title, what would it be?
5. What am I secretly proud of?
6. What's one thing I'm tolerating that I don't have to?
7. What did I learn about myself this week?
8. What's draining my energy — and what could I do about it?
9. What would I do if I weren't afraid?
10. Who or what made me smile today?
11. What's one tiny win I can celebrate?
12. When did I last feel truly at peace?
13. What am I pretending not to know?
14. What advice would I give my 10-year-younger self?
15. What's one thing I keep putting off — and why?
16. What part of today would I like to relive?
17. How am I really feeling — underneath the surface?

18. If I could write a letter to my future self, what would it say?

19. What's something I wish I had said — but didn't?

20. What am I clinging to that it might be time to release?

21. What's a belief I need to challenge?

22. What's one thing that would make tomorrow 10% better?

23. When do I feel most like myself?

24. What's something I need more of in my life right now?

25. What would I do differently if I knew nobody was watching?

26. What's the last thing I truly enjoyed — and how can I do more of it?

27. If my inner critic had a name, what would it be — and what would I say back?

28. What's a moment I want to remember from this week?

29. What story am I telling myself that might not be true?

30. What's one thing I've grown through, even if it hurt?

31. What do I need to hear today — and can I say it to myself?

And remember: you can always create your own prompts, too. In fact, the best ones often come from your own real questions. Don't worry about getting them "right" — if it gets you writing, it's working.

These are not epic questions meant to stir Shakespearean monologues. They are short, honest, deceptively simple questions that gently crack open the door to your inner world. Just enough for light to get in. And often, that's all it takes.

Think of one-line prompts as the espresso shots of journaling. Quick. Potent. Sometimes a little bitter. But they wake you up to something within.

Why They Work

Because we overthink. A lot. We think a "good" journal entry has to be profound or pretty. That it needs to have a beginning, middle, and a conclusion that would make a TED Talk proud.

But one-line prompts say: "Just answer me." That's it. No over-prep. No outlining. Just respond.

And often, the response surprises you. Like asking yourself, "What am I avoiding today?" and discovering it's not your inbox — it's a conversation you've been ducking. Or writing down, "What gave me energy this week?" and realizing it was that five-minute phone call with your friend where no one pretended.

Real-Life Examples:

- My friend Simran is a teacher and mom of two. She once told me the only time she gets to journal is during school pickup — while waiting in the car. She keeps a sticky note on her dashboard with just one line: *"What do I need more of right now?"* Her answers range from "quiet" to "vitamin D" to "my kids not screaming like goats today." It's raw. It's real. It works.

- Another example: Arjun, a mid-level manager, started using a simple question every Friday: *"What's one thing I did well this week?"* At first, he struggled. Then he wrote, "I actually listened to my team." That single sentence changed how he approached his leadership role — and his weekends.

- And me? I once answered the prompt *"What am I proud of today?"* with: "I watered my plants before they became a cautionary tale." It wasn't ground breaking, but it shifted my mood from shame to slight satisfaction — and sometimes, that's enough.

Great Prompts to Start With:

- "What made me laugh today?"
- "What am I not saying out loud?"
- "What's one thing I'm tired of pretending?"
- "Who made me feel seen this week?"
- "If my mood were a weather forecast, what would it be?"

These questions aren't meant to impress. They're meant to express. And sometimes, that's exactly what you need.

Make It a Ritual:

Want to turn this into a low-maintenance journaling habit? Set a timer for 5 minutes. Pick a prompt. Write until the timer buzzes. Stop.

That's it. No page goals. No judgment. You'll be amazed what happens when you remove pressure and just... respond.

And remember — your answer doesn't need to be long. Some days it may be a list. Other days, a single sentence. Occasionally, just a sigh and the word "UGH." (Valid.)

Pro Tip:

Make your own prompt list. Yes, borrow from others — but also listen to your life. What question keeps coming back to you in the shower, on walks, or when your head hits the pillow? Write it down. That's your prompt.

Because ultimately, the best prompts aren't the fancy ones. They're the ones that speak directly to the version of you that's reading this — a little tired, a little curious, and fully human.

So go ahead. Ask yourself something today.

And then, answer like nobody's watching. Because nobody is.

Just you. And the page.

Guided Templates: Routines That Keep You Anchored

Sometimes, what we need isn't a question — it's a rhythm. That's where guided templates come in. Think of them as the choreography of journaling. You don't need to invent new moves every day — you just follow the flow.

Morning Pages: Made famous by Julia Cameron's *The Artist's Way*, this technique involves writing three full pages of stream-of-consciousness every morning. No filter, no editing. It's a brain-dump, not a masterpiece.

Stream of consciousness is a journaling (or literary) technique where you write exactly what you're thinking, as you're thinking it — without editing, censoring, or organizing your thoughts. It's a raw, unfiltered flow of inner dialogue, like a mind dump on the page.

🧠 It often looks like this:

"I need to call Mum but maybe after lunch because I'm hungry and where did I put that to-do list and I hope the meeting isn't long and wow my desk is messy I should clean and why am I thinking about penguins right now…"

It's messy, meandering — and that's the point.

In journaling, **stream of consciousness** is helpful because:

- It bypasses your inner critic.

- It surfaces unconscious thoughts or feelings.

- It's therapeutic — a way to process thoughts without judgment.

It was made famous in literature by authors like Virginia Woolf and James Joyce, but in personal journaling, it's just a safe way to let your thoughts spill without worrying about grammar, structure, or making sense.

📖 Common stream-of-consciousness tools include:

- **Morning Pages**.

- **Timed writing** (e.g., "Write for 10 minutes nonstop — don't lift the pen").

- **Mind-dump journaling** (especially before bed to clear mental clutter).

Real-life example: A friend of mine used Morning Pages for six months and swears it helped him spot the storyline in his chaotic thoughts He also claims it's cheaper than therapy. (Not medically verified, but emotionally accurate.)

3-2-1 Format: For those who want structure without pressure:

- 3 things I'm grateful for
- 2 things I want to focus on today
- 1 thing I'm letting go of

Real-life example: A teacher named Preeti started her school day with this format. She once wrote "letting go of control" and ended up not flipping out when her whiteboard marker dried out mid-lecture. Progress!

The Sandwich Template:

- Top Slice: What's good right now?
- Filling: What's bothering me?
- Bottom Slice: What's one kind thing I can say to myself?

It's a journaling sandwich — emotional nourishment included. It helps you not spiral into rants without also forcing toxic positivity.

The Sunday Self-Check: Use this once a week:

- What felt meaningful this week?
- What drained me?
- What do I want more of next week?

You'd be surprised how helpful this is before planning your week. One reader told me she stopped scheduling 8 a.m. meetings just because her calendar said she was "free." Her journal told her she wasn't.

The Pep Talk Template:

- What's something hard I'm facing?
- What would I say to a friend going through this?
- Now say it to yourself.

Great for days when the inner critic is especially chatty.

Why Templates Work: They reduce friction. Instead of staring at a blank page wondering what to write, you just fill in the blanks. They also help you track emotional patterns over time.

Humorous Insight: One reader told me she used to write: "I'm grateful for coffee" every single day until she realized she wasn't grateful — she was addicted. She switched to "I'm grateful my brain is pretending to work."

The point is, templates add a scaffolding to your thoughts. They hold space for you to explore — gently, consistently, and creatively.

You don't have to reinvent the journaling wheel every day. Sometimes, a familiar format is all you need to roll forward.

Journaling on Autopilot (In a Good Way): A Chapter Recap

If you've ever sat down to journal and found yourself staring at the page like it personally betrayed you — this chapter was your antidote. Ditch the pressure to be profound and give yourself practical tools to keep your journaling habit fresh, fun, and ridiculously doable.

Begin with **daily prompts** — those single-line sparks that work like espresso shots for your mind. Whether it's *"What am*

I avoiding today?" or *"What made me laugh?"*, these questions get straight to the good stuff without making journaling feel like homework. The power lies in their simplicity — no long essays needed. Just one line. One moment. One honest check-in.

From there, we moved into **guided templates**, aka your journaling scaffolding. We met Morning Pages (hello, stream-of-consciousness brain dumps), and explored formats like the 3-2-1 method, the Sunday Self-Check, and even a Pep Talk Template that helps silence the inner critic. These aren't rules — they're rituals. They reduce decision fatigue and add rhythm to your reflection.

Real people shared real wins. Like Nisha, who discovered her job boredom through a one-line prompt. Or Preeti, a teacher who let go of control (and whiteboard marker tantrums) thanks to a simple structure. These stories reminded us that journaling doesn't have to be deep to be helpful — it just has to be honest.

The big idea? You don't need the perfect words. You need a way in. A container for your thoughts. Whether it's a jar of folded prompts, a gratitude sandwich, or just scribbles on a sticky note — this chapter reminded you that journaling is less about the *how* and more about the *showing up.*

So next time you feel stuck? Don't overthink. Just pick a prompt. Or follow a template. Or make up your own. Because the best journaling is the one that gets done.

Your Turn: A Week of Templates & Prompts

Ready to take all those new tools for a spin? This week, let's experiment — not with perfection, but with play. Try a **7-day journaling sampler,** using a different style each day. Each one takes **5–10 minutes max**, no candles or deep existential breakthroughs required (unless you want them).

📔 *Day 1: One-Line Prompt Jar*

Pull a prompt (use one from the list — or make your own!). Example:

"What made me feel most alive today?"

Write just 3–5 lines. That's enough.

📔 *Day 2: 3-2-1 Format*

- 3 things I'm grateful for
- 2 things I want to focus on today
- 1 thing I'm letting go of

📔 *Day 3: Sandwich Template*

- What's good right now?
- What's bothering me?
- One kind thing I can say to myself

(P.S. If it makes you hungry, that's okay too.)

📔 *Day 4: Stream-of-Consciousness*

Set a timer for 10 minutes. Write without stopping. No editing. No censoring. No making sense. Just write.

📔 *Day 5: Sunday Self-Check (even if it's Wednesday)*

- What felt meaningful this week?
- What drained me?

- What do I want more of next week?

📅 *Day 6: "If I Weren't Afraid..." Prompt*

Let this one surprise you. Write a few lines or a whole page. What might you do if fear wasn't driving the bus?

📅 *Day 7: Pep Talk to Yourself*

- What's hard right now?

- What would I say to a friend?

- Now say it to *me.*

📓 **Bonus Tip:** Keep it messy. Keep it honest. Doodle if you want. Miss a day? That's fine. This isn't school — it's your space to breathe.

Let the words come however they want. The important part? You showed up.

And that's what journaling — and growth — is really about.

Conclusion:
Your Journey Begins Here

Your Journey Begins Here

So here we are — not at the end, but at the edge of something powerful.

You've explored the "why," the "how," and the "what now" of journaling. You've seen that it doesn't take an hour a day or poetic brilliance. It just takes honesty, five minutes, and a pen. You've read stories of forgotten notebooks and triumphant comebacks. You've met your inner critic and your wiser self. And most importantly, you've begun a relationship — with your own thoughts.

This isn't the kind of practice that ends with the last page. It's the kind that begins with it.

Because journaling, at its core, is not about writing. It's about showing up.

It's about choosing to pause when the world rushes. To reflect when chaos calls. To listen — not to the noise around you, but to the voice within you.

And no, not every day will feel like a breakthrough. Some days you'll write half a sentence. Other days, your pen will surprise you. But each page you fill adds a thread to the tapestry of your self-understanding. It makes you more grounded, more resilient, and more *you*.

So go ahead — keep showing up.

Not perfectly. Not even daily (though better).

Just honestly.

You've built a journaling gym — now it's yours to return to, anytime, anywhere, in any state of mind.

The page is ready.

The question is simple:

Are you?

Happy journaling.

— Rajiv Krishnan Pisharoti

A Quiet Wish

I don't know where you'll be when you finish this book — maybe curled up on a couch, flipping through your journal, or halfway through a coffee in the middle of a noisy day.

But wherever you are, I have one simple wish for you:

That you keep showing up.

Not perfectly. Not every day. Just... when it matters. And it always matters more than we think.

In a world that constantly pushes us outward — to be faster, louder, busier — journaling is an inward act of quiet rebellion. It's how you reclaim a moment of truth in the middle of the noise.

I wrote this book not just to help you build a habit, but to give you a gentle reminder:

You already have everything you need — a mind that's curious, a heart that's felt, and a page that's waiting.

People try many things to stay light inside — therapy, meditation, yoga, affirmations, even herbal teas with names longer than the ingredients list. But journaling? It's simple. It's inexpensive. And it works.

It's also more than just emotional hygiene.

It's legacy.

It's self-respect.

It's mental and physical well-being — because let's face it, the two are deeply connected.

And maybe, just maybe, the more people sit down with themselves — honestly, patiently — the more we build a world that feels a little saner, a little kinder, a little more human.

So if this book nudged you even a little closer to the page, then it's done its job.

Now, go write something real.

Even if it's just: "I'm here."

Because that's always a powerful place to begin.

Happy journaling.

— Rajiv Krishnan Pisharoti

Thank You

To every reader who turned the pages, picked up a pen, scribbled in the margins, or simply paused for a breath — thank you.

Writing this book was an act of love. Reading it, reflecting with it, and living with it? That's what brings it to life.

You didn't just read a book.

You took a small but powerful step toward meeting yourself more honestly.

And for that, I'm deeply grateful.

Stay curious. Stay kind.

And if your journal ever feels too quiet — just know, somewhere out there, mine's quietly open too.

— *Rajiv Krishnan Pisharoti*

"Every reader's journey is unique. If The Journaling Gym made a difference in yours, I'd be grateful to hear from you at babasrajiv@gmail.com."

 Acknowledgements

No book is ever written in isolation — even the most introspective journaling journeys are quietly supported by the hearts, minds, and moments shared with others.

To Rajyogi Brahma Kumar Nikunj Ji — Sir, it was your inspiration that helped me begin, and more importantly, return to the precious habit of journaling. Your many talks — where this subject would gently yet powerfully emerge — acted as reminders to realign myself with this reflective practice. Despite your immense commitments, including authoring over 9000 published articles for national and international newspapers — a monumental feat — and rendering tireless service to humanity through the Brahma Kumaris, you always encouraged me to write this book. I place on record my deepest gratitude not only for your blessings to me, but also for the light you continue to shine on countless lives across the world.

To my wife, Smitha — your boundless patience and quiet strength carried me through this process. I owe you far more than these acknowledgements; I owe you half the book.

To my son, Rohan — thank you for the valuable insights and thoughtful perspectives you so generously offered.

To my dear friend, Shekhar Atreya — you were vacationing in London, and yet found time to read the draft of this book and send me valuable suggestions. Your generosity and belief in this work moved me deeply. Thank you for walking beside me, even from across continents.

To every person who trusted me with their stories of journaling — thank you for your honesty. Your reflections gave this book its depth, its humour, and its soul.

To my readers — you, who chose to embrace a book that offered not productivity, but presence — I am deeply grateful. Your willingness to pause, pick up a pen, and reconnect with yourself on the page is the true spirit behind this work.

To my dear friends Abraham Verghese and Rekha Abraham Verghese in Gurugram — I am profoundly thankful for your encouragement and advice, all the more meaningful given the demands on your own time.

To Roma Rakesh Menon, Vijaya Rakesh Menon, and Rakesh Gopal Menon — thank you for reviewing the draft and sharing your thoughtful feedback from Singapore, despite the challenges of time zones and your respective professional commitments.

To my extended circle of friends and family — thank you for believing in this journey, for cheering me on during late nights, detours, and countless revisions.

To each one of you — thank you, from the bottom of my heart.

With deep gratitude,

Rajiv Krishnan Pisharoti

9 798889 069994